GW01086744

Date of Return

-9 JUN 1989

SEP 1984

6 APR 1988

NOV 1993

16 AUG

Molly Came First

Molly

Molly
Came First

Mary Rose FBHS

Illustrated by Joan Thompson

Harrap London

TO AMANDA, ANTHONY, AND COLIN; MARK, JOANNA,
CHRISTOPHER, AND SIMON; AND HOWARD, MARTIN,
JULIA AND THOMAS WITH VERY MUCH LOVE

First published in Great Britain 1978
by GEORGE G. HARRAP & CO. LTD
182 High Holborn, London WC1V 7AX

Text © *Mary Rose* 1978
Illustrations © *George G. Harrap & Co. Ltd* 1978

All rights reserved. No part of this
publication may be reproduced in any
form or by any means without the prior
permission of George G. Harrap & Co. Ltd

ISBN 0 245 53259 5

Designed by Leslie & Lorraine Gerry

Illustrated by Joan Thompson of The Garden Studio

Filmset by Woolaston Parker Ltd., Leicester

Printed in Great Britain by offset lithography by
Biddles Ltd, Guildford

Foreword

This is a true story, mainly about a very remarkable pony, but it is also the story of two little girls. Of course, they are not little now: in fact they were always rather tall for their age, and this made the choice of a pony for them rather difficult. Mary and Philippa (Pip) always wanted a pony – in spite of an almost unmentionable incident when I foolishly sat Mary on the back of a horse at the age of three. I should have understood that even a small horse must look enormous to a little girl, and any parent reading this will, I hope, let their children get really used to ponies before lifting them up and putting them on the animals' backs.

Before buying a pony for our young daughters, however, we wanted them to learn something about how to handle and look after ponies, and the only person nearby who could teach them this was a very remarkable old lady named Miss Doerring. She had taught riding to many army officers and still owned a few horses and ponies which lived on Port Meadow. Miss Doerring began her lessons by teaching her pupils to ride bareback, without a saddle, and usually without a bridle. At most, the pupils were allowed a rope from a headcollar or halter, and in this way they learnt balance and how to control a pony without pulling at its head or hurting its mouth.

Much of the lesson was spent doing exercises on the pony's back, both standing still and on the lunge at walk and trot, and later at canter too, and these exercises developed the necessary muscles in the rider, at the same time instilling a proper sense of balance and great confidence. At the end of a lesson either Mary or Pip might be allowed to ride the horse on which they had been having their lesson back to its herd, and I remember on one occasion Philippa being turned loose on Great Girl, a beautiful chestnut ex-steeplechaser 16.2 h.h. At first Great Girl walked quietly beside the pony which Miss Doerring was leading but soon she seemed to become excited with the idea of getting back to her companions and started to canter. Pip's mother and I watched anxiously as she was borne away from us, expecting to see her fall to the ground at almost every stride; however, she held Great Girl's mane and was carried to the herd, which consisted mostly of unbroken young carthorses, and then we really did get worried because these young horses began to canter about and kick with high spirits and pleasure at having their friend back. Pip was not in the least worried and slid down from her mount's back and made her way safely out of the mêlée and back to us across the meadow.

Not long after this we learnt that a riding school was starting up in Wolvercote (near Oxford) and we decided that the girls should have some more orthodox riding lessons and the opportunity of hiring horses to ride on the meadow; and that as they were so keen, their mother and I decided that we, too, should have lessons so that we could share their pleasure in riding and not be entirely ignorant when they went to shows.

There were several horses and ponies in the yard at the new riding school and it took a little time for us to get to know them, but it soon became evident that there was a real 'character' in the yard and that she was a favourite with everyone who went there to ride. This pony was Molly, but I must leave Mary to tell you about her.

W. Robert Rose
April 1978

Contents

LIBRARY

Illustrations

The Schedule   1

The schedule arrived early in April. It was quite a small, folded, printed sheet and it announced that the Oxfordshire Young Farmers' Club would hold their first Horse Show and Gymkhana on a date towards the end of August that year. It had been addressed to 'The Misses Rose' and Pip and I read it breathlessly, almost with disbelief. It was our first schedule! Pip voiced the thought uppermost in both our minds.

'We must have a pony in time to enter,' she said.

Pip was ten and I was nearly twelve years old, and we had wanted a pony desperately for years and years. We had been having regular riding lessons from a private instructor for the past six years, and just recently, we had been allowed to go to a local riding school to help at week-ends and to have some jumping lessons. But it wasn't the same as having our own pony.

It was at the riding school that we met Molly. She was a dark brown pony mare, 13.2 h.h. and admitted to being twelve years old, but later on, after we had bought her, the vet told us that this was probably about half her true age.

Molly was known around the stables as a 'Welsh type pony' but her breeding was probably rather mixed up and she did not look at all like the Welsh Mountain ponies we knew, nor was she heavily built like the Welsh Cobs. She had good bone, but very little 'feather' (hair round the fetlock joint found on horses of common, or mixed, ancestry) and she was narrow across the back which made her easy for a child to sit astride. She had a very broad white blaze, in the shape of a cross, which covered the whole of the front of her face. The blaze was so unusual and so distinctive that Pip and I were secretly convinced that Molly must be a descendant of one of the War Horses used at the time of the Crusades. There is a legend, which we had heard when we were very young, that tells how the Christians bred horses specially with huge white blazes in the shape of the cross so that, in the heat of a battle, they could easily distinguish their own soldiers and not kill each other by mistake.

Molly showed other signs of good blood in her ancestry – she had a finely chiselled, rather 'dish' face, with wide-apart eyes and large delicate nostrils; a very fine silky black mane and a long, well-shaped black tail. She also had an unexpected turn of speed for a pony her size. However, it was her personality rather than her looks which singled her out from the common herd of horses. Molly cared about people – she was an energetic, active ride for a good rider, yet she would walk about very slowly and carefully if a tiny child was placed on her back. If some boastful, over-confident teenager jumped on her wanting to show off to his friends, she would take off at a fast run and stop suddenly, giving a little buck if necessary and deposit her rider in the dirt; but if her rider lacked confidence and was hesitant in giving Molly directions, she would behave herself beautifully, carrying her rider smoothly and with great consideration. Other horses might be more beautiful, or younger, or better trained, but in all the world there was only one Molly.

After we received the horse show schedule, Pip and I went all out towards our one and only desire – getting a pony. By July we had just about won our battle. Our parents couldn't stand our entreaties, tantrums, wheedling or cajoling any longer and agreed to let us buy Molly between us with our own savings,

10

saying that they would help us out with any extra money we needed.

Michael, our elder brother, was away at boarding school most of the time, but we knew he had £10 in the Post Office and Pip and I had about £5 each. We decided for Michael that he would spend his £10 on Molly (which he gallantly did). This meant we had to 'borrow' £10 from our parents, as Molly was for sale for £30 complete with saddle and bridle. If this seems incredibly cheap to you, please remember that this was 1948 and a pound then was worth a great deal more than it is today! In fact, the saddle proved to be useless, so our poor parents had to foot the bill for a new saddle as well.

As the end of that summer term drew near, the excitement in our home built steadily up to fever pitch. We were to be allowed to buy Molly at the beginning of the summer holidays and no other subject of conversation or thought seemed able to penetrate to us. Examinations came and went, and the last day of term. And then disaster struck! We were playing in a corner of the college playing fields next to our house one evening right at the beginning of August. We were going to fetch Molly at the week-end and were wildly happy. It was an overcast, thundery day and every so often heavy rain emptied down so that the streets were running with water. We were playing a most absorbing game, called 'blind pit ponies'. I was the blind pit pony and Pip was my master, which meant that I had to go about with my eyes shut and she drove me with two long pieces of string. When we heard Mother calling us in to supper we were so pleased with our game that instead of climbing the fence, as usual, we decided to gallop round by the gate and come home along the road, to prolong our fun.

'Coming, coming!' we yelled, and then set off, full pelt across the field; I with my eyes tight shut and Pip grasping the string for dear life. Through the gate and then along the pavement we raced. Round the corner, and then . . . crash! I caught my foot in a rough patch of pavement and came sprawling to the ground. Unfortunately, there was a lamp-post in my way, the sort with a little ridge round it about three feet from the ground, and I hit this ridge slap on my nose! The lamp-post bears a dent to this day!

I lay perfectly still for a second and waves of horror chilled my bones. Only a few more days and Molly would be ours and I had to go and do something idiotic like this. I struggled quickly to my feet and clasped my streaming nose with my hand. There was blood everywhere and Pip was so stunned she couldn't even speak, but just trotted meekly behind me as I ran home.

'Mummy, Mummy!' I called, bursting into the house. 'I fell over and hit a lamp-post – my nose isn't broken, is it? It can't be broken, it's just bleeding, isn't it?'

'Oh, no Dear, I don't think it's broken,' Mother lied soothingly. I shall never know how she managed to keep her voice so calm and matter of fact when faced with a very grimy, bloody, child with an obviously shattered nose, but she did.

'I think we had better take you to the hospital, all the same' she added, as she went to the telephone to call a taxi. 'Philippa, you and Michael have your tea. It's all ready, we shall not be very long' Mother said calmly as she picked up her mackintosh and hand bag. 'Come along, Dear' she turned to me, 'the taxi has just arrived.'

If I had been thinking straight I would have wondered why she didn't even attempt to wash the blood away but just handed me a huge damp cloth to hold to my nose and wiped my hands a bit clean, but I felt quite sure that everything would be all right and nothing would come between myself and Molly's imminent arrival. We went out to the taxi and just as we were getting into it my Father arrived home from his office. He took in the grimy scene at once, leaned his bicycle up against the wall, and got into the taxi with us to come to the hospital.

When we arrived at the Radcliffe Infirmary I suppose we went through all the normal out-patients procedure, but I remember little of it. A Doctor looked at my nose and gave me an injection which froze it so I didn't feel any pain, and I was too drowsy to protest much when my parents went away and left me in a clean white bed in an antiseptic smelling ward. It was not an unpleasant ward and everyone was very kind and I was very sleepy! The next day the Doctor put my nose in a plaster splint, but said that he couldn't set it because it was too badly crushed, and anyway, the bones of the nose do not mature until you are about 17 so it was very difficult to set a child's nose. I would just have to wear this mask-like plaster on my face for a couple of weeks and hope for the best.

Now I really began to fret. The days in hospital seemed interminable and I was terrified that they wouldn't allow me to go home in time for the week-end when Molly was to be fetched. But I was fortunate and the Doctor let me out after four days, on condition that I stayed quietly in bed at home for another day or two.

So it was that on that sunny Sunday morning when Pip rode Molly from the riding school at Wolvercote, down Port Meadow and up the road to our house, I was in my bedroom, overlooking the back garden. Pip brought Molly into the pocket-handkerchief-sized front garden, along the narrow passage beside the house, through the tall 'back' gate and into our narrow strip of back garden. There was a path down the centre and vegetables (remnants of our war effort) on one side of the path and a grassy patch, which was referred to rather grandly as 'the lawn' on the other. The bottom of the garden was fenced off right across and totally taken up by a chicken house and run.

I looked out of my bedroom window and saw Pip sitting on Molly's back while the mare grazed happily on the lawn. The sun was shining and everyone was outside making a fuss of Molly. I could smell the lunch cooking and I felt very miserable and alone because I was stuck upstairs and all this was going on without me, so I put on some shoes and a dressing gown over my pyjamas and went downstairs and out into the garden.

13

'Whatever are you doing out here' Mother asked, not unkindly, as I appeared, trying to look very nonchalant.

'Well, I just wanted to say hello to Molly' I said, in a rather dejected voice.

'Oh well, I don't suppose a little fresh air and sunshine will do you any harm' said Father.

'Wouldn't you like to sit on Molly for a bit?' said Pip, and slid easily to the ground.

'Oh, yes!' I scrambled quickly onto Molly's back in case anyone decided it might be bad for me to ride before I got a chance to sit on her. She felt wonderful. Suddenly I was lord of the whole world. I could hear the lovely summer sounds again and feel the warmth of the sunshine on my shoulders and the living strength beneath me, and smell the crushed grass under Molly's hooves. I rode her up and down the path a couple of times and then dismounted and patted her and returned to my bedroom without too much fuss. I was quite happy now; by tomorrow I would be out and about again and there would be Molly, and all the excitement of practising for the gymkhana, and endless rides across the Meadow – and no more games of blind pit ponies, ever!

At Last – A Pony! 2

During the next few weeks Pip and I spent a good deal of time practising gymkhana events on Molly. We set off from the house straight after breakfast with a bridle and some titbits, and walked down to Port Meadow where Molly lived, by arrangement with the Riding School. The Meadow was 500 acres of Common land just north of Oxford. It was about a mile and a half long and half a mile or more wide, and almost completely flat, bordered on one long side by the river Thames and on the other by some allotments and the railway line. It was, of course, very low lying land and most of it was flooded for about half the year – perhaps because of this, and the fact that a large number of cattle were grazed there with the horses, it was extremely good and rich pasture. Sometimes we might have to walk almost to the far end to find Molly, but we never minded this; we talked and planned endlessly together about how we were going to train her, what classes we would each ride in at the horse show, and so on.

All the horses on the Meadow lived in small groups or herds. There was very little movement between the herds, once a horse was accepted into a particular herd it generally stayed with that herd. We quickly got to know all the horses on the Meadow and all the herds, so that even when we couldn't see Molly from a distance we might be able to spot another horse from her herd and so could at least walk in the right direction and not waste ages wandering all over the Meadow looking for her. We soon learnt the favourite haunts of each herd and where we would be most likely to find Molly and her herd at any particular time of day or in any particular type of weather.

Having found Molly our troubles had only just begun. We then had to catch her! If you have ever tried to catch a wily old pony in the middle of a 500 acre meadow when the pony did not wish to be caught, you will know all the difficulties and heartbreaks involved, and if you have not, then I sincerely hope that you will never have to undergo this particular type of torture. I don't think it's quite so maddening if the horse you are after takes flight and gallops right to the far end of the meadow. At least then you have time for contemplation whilst walking all the way back to try again, but Molly used to play games with us unmercifully. Sometimes she would allow us to walk straight up to her, would accept the proffered apple or carrot and stand like a statue so that we could put on her bridle and jump on her back; but much more often, she would let us walk up really close and then, when she was still just out of reach, she would turn and walk away a few paces. She might even take the bribe out of our hands before jumping back. She was extremely cunning and had the whole procedure worked out almost to a fine art. She would walk round us in a small circle, and if we showed any sign of increasing our speed from a slow walk, which was the pace we had been taught to use when approaching ponies, Molly would still keep beyond our grasp by breaking into a gentle trot. She seldom ran away, however, but would trot round and round, maddeningly, so near, and yet so far.

The game of catch did have certain rules, however, which, fortunately, Molly accepted, and one of these rules was that if we succeeded in touching her, we had won, and she would stand still to be caught. Touching her included catching hold of her tail, since she was far too much of a lady to dream of

We now had to catch Molly

kicking out. So, in moments of desperation, one of us might be seen making a frantic dive at Molly's tail as she trotted round in a circle, just out of reach of the other! Another of Molly's favourite pranks was to wade out into the river until the water was above the level of her knees, when she grew bored with trotting round us, and there she would stand, head pointing out to mid-stream, laughing at us – but not for long! We very quickly learnt how to vault on her from behind without getting our feet wet, by taking a flying leap from the bank!

We seldom rode Molly with a saddle because it was such a nuisance having to carry it so far and then carry it about all over the Meadow, as we could never be sure how long it would take us to find her. In fact, we were taught to ride bareback and hardly rode on a saddle at all during the first five or six years of our riding lives, so we didn't miss it at all. We infinitely preferred riding bareback as we were so much closer to our horse and could feel the movement of the muscles under the lovely silky coat and the warmth of Molly's friendly body. Quite often we rode without a bridle, too, perhaps with a piece of string around Molly's nose, but sometimes we simply guided her with our legs or by pushing her head round the way we wanted to go with a hand on the opposite side of her neck. She was a most obliging pony and not the type who would stop and graze when being ridden, and since her mouth had long since been ruined by use in the riding school, we could stop her just as well without a bit, possibly better.

How much gymkhana work Molly had ever done before we did not know, so during the first few days that we had her we practised quite hard. It wasn't so easy to find poles to 'bend' round, so we used willow twigs about three or four feet long which stuck easily into the soft ground and pretended they were tall straight poles. Usually we would erect a row of five or six and then take it in turns to ride Molly down them, weaving in and out between the poles which were set about 8 yards apart. We started by trotting in and out down the row of poles but we knew that we would have to canter if we were ever to get into a final, so very soon we started practising at a canter. Molly was grand and as soon as she had got the hang of the game she whizzed along and spun round the end pole, turning on a sixpence so that she wasted as little time as possible before returning to the starting point, still going between the poles. We were very strict about not tiring Molly out and not doing any one game for too long in case she got bored. We were also scrupulously fair about sharing her and always worked out our turns on her to the last yard.

Pip and I had only been to a couple of horse shows or gymkhanas in our lives and we didn't know a great deal about them from first hand experience, but we had read so many 'pony' books that I think we knew every game ever invented, and how best to train our pony to perform efficiently on the day. There was a very popular race called the potato race in which about six potatoes were placed on the ground at the far end of the ring and a bucket placed at the starting line. All the competitors lined up by their buckets and on the word 'go' they all set off at a gallop to the far end, dismounted, picked up a potato, remounted, and galloped back to their bucket, dropped the potato into it whilst still mounted, and then set off for the next potato. This was one of the games we intended to enter on the 'great day' and it was obvious that we must practise jumping on at the canter if we were to get anywhere in it, as well as throwing potatoes into buckets whilst Molly was still moving. Even without any buckets or potatoes we practised jumping on at the canter, which is not difficult once you know how, but does demand agility and a good sense of balance.

Only a few days after we had got Molly, when I still had my nose in plaster, I was trying this jumping on at the canter in one of our favourite corners of the Meadow. I took too big a jump and swung myself right over to the other side, landing heavily on my head. The turf was soft but even so the jarring was terrific and I lay still, convinced I had broken my neck. After all, I did seem to be a bit accident prone at the time! Pip was horrified to see me lying so still and was quite relieved to find I could still speak. Somehow she bundled me up on top of Molly and led me all the way home. It was a long silent journey, but by the time we did, eventually reach the front gate, I had decided that, in fact, it was unlikely that I had broken my neck because I thought that if I had done so I would have been dead by then, so we decided to say nothing to Mother in case she stopped us practising for the gymkhana. It was quite usual for us to bring Molly back to the house at lunch times (we tied her up in the back garden with a bucket of oats, mixed with carrots, potato peelings, or cabbage leaves, which she simply loved) but Mother must have been suspicious that day because we were unusually silent and I remember sitting quite still in the dining room for simply ages trying to decide just what damage I had done to my head and neck after all! By the time we had finished lunch I had completely recovered and Pip and I set off for the Meadow once again, but from then on we were a good deal more careful how we rode.

Molly was an excellent schoolmistress. She seemed to know instinctively when someone sat on her back what was required. You could quite safely put a tiny baby on her and she would walk about so carefully that the baby could not possibly fall. But if a rather cocky teenager got on her with the intention of showing off she would either take the bit between her teeth and gallop flat out across the Meadow and then buck them off, or she would trot very fast in a straight line and suddenly swerve to the right or left dropping her shoulder at the same time, so that her rider was deposited ignominiously on the turf. With a nervous beginner, child or adult, she was gentle, docile, and incredibly obedient so that she gave her rider tremendous confidence, but once she knew they were fairly steady on top she conveniently forgot her good manners and more or less went where she chose at the pace she chose. If, however, her rider did come unstuck, Molly always stood quite still beside them ready to be remounted, and I cannot remember her ever running away when someone fell off her. She was very wise, completely ignored all traffic, and had unbounded love and patience which she bestowed on all the human race, but particularly on children. Pip and I would often sit underneath her whilst she grazed on a hot summer afternoon, so that we had the benefit of the shade she made with her body, and we were never in the slightest danger of being stepped on or kicked by Molly, who had evidently assumed the self-imposed task of being our guardian and protector.

A Visit to the Blacksmith 3

Every day, when we took Molly home to lunch, we groomed her carefully with a dandy brush to remove all the mud and dirt from her coat and keep her skin healthy and clean. We gently brushed out her mane and tail, which were fine and not at all bushy, showing some Thoroughbred or Arab blood in her ancestry. We knew that to use a body brush on her would have been wrong because its fine, close-set hairs would have removed the protective grease from her coat and left her without her natural 'rainproofing' but we were sure she appreciated her daily dandy brushing. We also sponged her eyes and nose and her dock, and picked the mud out of her feet with a hoofpick.

It was when Molly had been in the family about three weeks that we noticed one day that she had a loose shoe. We knew from books that ponies needed re-shoeing about every six weeks because even if their shoes weren't worn out or loose, their feet grew all the time and would have become long enough in six weeks to require trimming back. But it was one thing knowing something from a book and quite a different matter trying to decide whether Molly's feet were long enough to need trimming, whether the clenches of the nails had risen, and the shoe become too small. After considerable discussion we decided that it was time Molly paid a visit to the blacksmith,

Unshod horse's foot

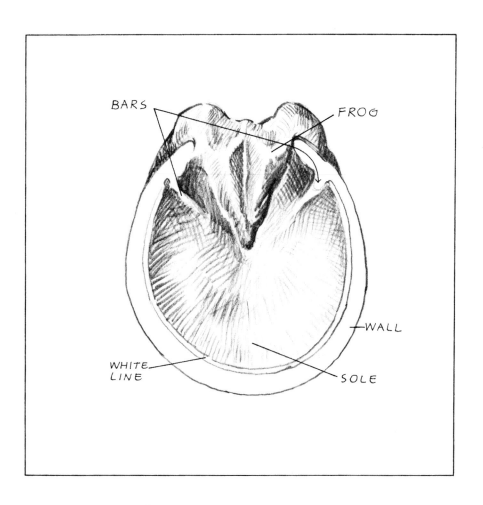

but as this was one of the aspects of being pony owners we hadn't previously considered, we didn't know how to go about finding a good blacksmith within hacking distance.

Mother came to the rescue, and after spending some time telephoning, she told us that she had made an appointment for Molly with a Mr. Slater who had his forge only about two miles from our house, near the old city jail in Oxford. We had never actually been to the forge, but we knew whereabouts it was because we had, at one time, had ballet dancing classes in a house in the same road. So, on the appointed day, at the beginning of the next week, we caught Molly early, took her home, brushed her and, just for a change, saddled her, and then set off towards the town. We did not have to go along the main road into town to get to the old city prison, but followed the back streets and kept away from the worst of the traffic. Molly obediently walked along at her swinging pace, stood patiently at the traffic lights and completely ignored the cars and buses and lorries. As always, we took it in turns to ride her – the other one being mounted on the faithful bicycle.

When we reached the forge we were relieved to see the big double doors already open and to hear the sound of a hammer on the anvil. We had hoped to arrive early as we knew blacksmiths were very busy people and that they shouldn't be kept waiting. I got off the bicycle and pushed it cautiously through the doors. The yard looked grey and dismal, the high wall cutting off most of the light. There were stacks of old rusty iron here and there, an old van parked over to the left and, on the right, a wooden shelter, consisting of a roof and two walls and open at the front. Inside the shelter stood a big grey cart-horse. He was tied to the wall at the back of the shed but had turned his head curiously at the sound of Molly's hooves, ears pricked, eyes alert. The man standing at the anvil was short and rather stocky, his brown hair was turning grey at the sides and his brown eyes looked at me from behind horn-rimmed spectacles. In one huge hand he held his blacksmith's hammer and he was hammering at the horseshoe he held on the anvil in a giant pair of pincers.

'Oh, come on in, Missey' he said when he saw me. 'You must be the Rose girls, and this is the pony your Mother telephoned about' he added, as Pip and Molly came through the gates. 'I've nearly finished this old boy, won't keep you waiting long'. Pip dismounted, ran the stirrup irons up the leathers and loosened Molly's girth, and then we moved up as close as we dared to the anvil to watch the final shoe being put on the grey horse.

We had never been in a blacksmith's forge before and we were fascinated by the whole business. As soon as he had finished the grey horse, Mr. Slater moved him over to one side of the shed and told us to bring Molly inside. It had just started to rain so we were quite glad to be under cover. Mr. Slater tied Molly up to the ring in the wall so that we didn't have to hold her and could watch exactly what he did. He picked up Molly's left front foot and held it between his knees. Pip was just a little apprehensive about the whole thing. 'You won't hurt her, will you?' she asked a little anxiously as Mr. Slater took his hammer and buffer and set to work cutting off all the clenches so that he could pull the shoe off without tearing the horn.

'Now Miss, don't you worry. This won't hurt the little mare at all. You watch me and I'll show you how we do it. See this foot? Well, all this outside part is made of horn and doesn't feel anything, just like your finger nails, only much thicker. The wall, that's the bit you see when the foot is on the ground, and this sole that you can see here now I've picked her foot up,' (he tapped the sole of Molly's foot gently with his hammer) 'this sole is hard and horny. It protects her sensitive foot that's inside this horny hoof from injury from stony ground and so on. See how it's slightly concave, like a saucer turned upside down? That's to give her a better grip on the ground, make her sure footed. And see this peculiar wedge-shaped part – know what that's called?'

'Yes,' we both said, 'that's the frog.'

25

'That's right.' Mr. Slater seemed pleased to have two eager students to talk to and was evidently prepared to elaborate considerably; and we were so fascinated we didn't mind if he talked all afternoon.

'Well, this here frog is made of horn, too. Softer kind of horn than the wall for instance, but horn just the same. It's an anti-slipping device and also like a sort of shock absorber. It makes contact with the ground first when your pony puts her foot down and all the shock of the impact of the foot on the ground is taken first of all by the frog. Your pony's got good feet, good big frog, good horn. Inside the foot, you see, there's a sort of cushion under the frog and that spreads the shock out sideways a bit so that the leg doesn't have to suffer such severe jarring.'

All the time he was talking Mr. Slater had been busy with hammer and buffer and when he had carefully cut all the clenches off he picked up his huge pincers and started to lever the shoe off. He took hold of the heels first and the shoe seemed to come away quite easily and was soon only attached at the toe. One final swift movement and the shoe was off, leaving Molly's foot fully visible.

'Now I have to prepare this foot for the new shoe,' said Mr. Slater affably. 'First of all we cut away some of the overgrowth of horn because the wall keeps on growing all the time. If she wasn't shod, of course, that would get worn away a little bit each day by just walking about, but the shoe stops the horn of the wall touching the ground so I have to cut it away a bit.' He took up his horn cutters, which looked just like pincers but had a flat piece where the two cutting edges joined. He clipped a semi-circle of horn off the hoof all the way round. Then he took up a strange looking knife that he told us was called a 'drawing knife' and trimmed up the ragged parts of the sole and frog.

'Good blacksmith never cuts away at the sole of a horse's foot' he announced. 'You only just have to trim up any raggedy bits, like I'm doing now. Now I'll just rasp it to make quite sure the surface is level.' A few swift strokes with the rasp seemed to

26

satisfy him and he gently let Molly's foot back down onto the ground and looked at it critically. 'See that?' he said. 'A good, well shaped foot. Nice and trim and all level ready for the new shoe!'

We watched, fascinated, as Mr. Slater went through exactly the same performance with each of Molly's feet and then he moved over to the far side of the shed where his furnace was glowing dimly. He pumped away at the bellows for a bit and soon the embers leapt into life and his fire was blazing. He had taken down a set of shoes from a nail on the wall and now put two of them into the fire.

'I make all my own shoes,' he said 'but I make them in the evenings when I'm not too busy and keep a stock of more or less standard sizes. Then I can just trim them to each individual foot when the time comes.' He showed us the shoes he was going to put on Molly. 'There are dozens of different types of shoes' he said, 'but these are about the best sort for you to have on your pony for the work you do with her. These are like the shoes I would put on a hunter, only smaller, and they help your pony to move fast on grass and pull up quickly and turn, and so on. See how they're made? That's called 'concave iron' when the part of the shoe that will be against the pony's foot is wider than the surface which will be in contact with the ground – that reduced the risk of suction in soft going and gives a better grip on the ground. And see this groove round the ground surface? That's called 'fullering' – makes a good place for the nails and gives a better foothold. And look at the heels. I don't just leave them cut off roughly, they are tapered almost to a smooth point; that's called 'pencilled heels' and I do that so there's less risk of her treading on the heels of her front shoes with her hind feet and pulling a shoe off. If you look at the hind shoes you'll see I've 'rolled' the toe. See, it's set back a little bit and bevelled off, for the same reason.'

By now the two front shoes in the fire were glowing red hot and Mr. Slater picked out the right one with his pincers, took it to the anvil, banged it about a bit and then stuck a pritchell into one of the nail holes so that he could carry it without having to get his hand too near the hot iron, and came back to where we were standing beside Molly. He picked up her foot and held the red hot shoe against the horn, trying it for size. Immediately, the forge was filled with thick, acrid, smoke and the most distinctive odour of burning horn. We peered at Molly's smoking hoof and wondered how on earth Mr. Slater could tell if the shoe fitted through all that smoke! Every few seconds he hissed through his teeth, blowing the smoke aside for a brief moment and apparently he was able to tell where the shoe needed adjustment for he carried it back to the anvil and hammered at it some more, fitted it again, and, when he was eventually satisfied with the fit, he dropped the shoe into a tank of water that stood beside the anvil where it hissed and spat whilst the water cooled it.

The blacksmith went through the same procedure with Molly's other front foot and then brought the two completed shoes over and nailed them on with sure, swift strokes of his hammer. We noticed that he put four nails in on the outside and three on the inside and quite a lot of the nail came out about a third of the way up the wall of Molly's hoof. As soon as he had banged all the nails well in, he drew her foot forwards and deftly twisted off the sharp ends of all the nails, and then hammered down the clenches, holding his pincers under the head of the nail at the same time to ensure a tight fit. He then tapped the toe clip lightly back into position, and finally ran his rasp round the extremity of the wall where the horn and the shoe met. He soon had both front feet finished, and then he started fitting the hind shoes in exactly the same way.

Soon Molly was standing proudly on four new shoes looking very smug, and Mr. Slater finished off the job by oiling her feet for us with some hoof oil. That made her look terribly smart and we were extra proud of her as we rode happily home. We felt we'd learnt a lot and also made a new friend in Mr. Slater, as he waved us a cheery farewell from his gateway.

28

The Horse Show   4

The lovely August days passed quickly and we spent all of them
happily out on Port Meadow with Molly, only coming home as
dusk began to creep across the sky. We knew and loved the
Meadow; we knew where it would be wet and where the ground
was firm; we knew where there was shelter to be found from the
wind or the occasional rain; we knew the river and we used to
ride Molly in the shallows, watching the sunlight on the
churned water as she ploughed through it. Sometimes we were
allowed to go swimming in the river and then we liked to ride
Molly into the water, until she was swimming, and swim
alongside her or float by her clinging on to her mane. I will not
pretend that we never quarrelled over her, but on the whole I
think we accepted the fact that she was to be shared, and, after
all, looking at her was almost as good as riding her – she was so
beautiful!

One day, when we had Molly in the garden and were
preparing her for the show, which was now only a few days off,
by trimming the little bits of feather from her heels, pulling her
mane and straightening up the rather straggly bottom of her
tail, Philippa had a brainwave. She had seen pictures of clipped
horses who appeared to have a sort of inverted V shape at the
top of their tails which made them look as if their tails were set
on a little higher. She didn't realize that this effect was obtained

by clipping the horse and leaving a V of hair at the top of the tail, and she determined that Molly should have this smart-looking trim for the show. So, when Mike and I had gone into lunch, she stayed outside with the scissors and when we went out again afterwards to saddle up for the afternoon ride, we saw that Molly's hindquarters bore a ragged V of clipped hair over her tail. Poor Pip, it is not at all easy to cut a V into the summer coat of a pony with a pair of blunt scissors and, all things considered, she had really not done too bad a job! But I was furious and really let fly at her for chopping poor Molly about. Whilst I worked myself into a state of frenzy over the disfigurement, Molly stood passively by, smiling gently as always. She knew that the hair would grow again in a month or two, even if we didn't!

Miss Doerring, our riding instructor, had taught us to ride bareback and didn't really believe in using saddles and bridles, so one of the things we more or less had to teach ourselves was how to clean and care for tack. Our first efforts at this were not altogether successful. Even before Molly arrived, we had determined that *our* pony was going to have the best of everything – she would be looked after, fed, groomed and schooled absolutely perfectly, and she would never, never have dirty tack (which we considered to be a dreadful insult to that noble animal the horse). However, it was rather easier said than done, and after Pip and I had struggled manfully for about an hour, she with the saddle and I with the bridle, we were horrified to find that the leather was inches deep in a foamy lather!

The violent argument which inevitably ensued brought Mother to the scene of our troubles; she, too, was rather dismayed when she saw the awful mess which was supposed to be our clean tack. After reading the instructions on the tin of saddle soap, she told us both to stop yelling at each other and start all over again on the tack. When we had washed it, apparently, we had made it much too wet, so Mother said we had better wash it again with almost dry sponges to remove all the surplus lather as well as all the dirt and grease, and then gently rub the saddle soap in, again with a sponge that was very nearly dry. So, rather subdued, we started once again on the tack, and about an hour later we had produced quite a creditable result. Certainly it had taken us a long time (we were very thorough and had taken everything to pieces carefully cleaning each buckle and the snaffle bit with Silvo and washing and soaping in the parts where the leather folded double to pass round the bit and into the buckles). But looking at our handiwork we felt it had been worth it. After a little practice we became quite proficient at tack cleaning and we really enjoyed doing it. If we couldn't actually be with Molly in the evenings, then cleaning her tack was the next best thing.

At last the day of the Horse Show arrived. We got up terribly early and went down to the Meadow to catch Molly. I loved the walk down to the Meadow in the early morning – the sun had not been up long and the whole world looked fresh and new. Now, in late August, there was already a hint of coming Autumn in the air which sharpened our pleasure in the remaining weeks of summer. The willow trees bordering the canal towing path, along which we walked, were thick and green, and the hedgerow smelt of high summer. The pale sky was mirrored in the still water of the canal, and we were glad that it wasn't particularly bright and sunny.

Just for once Molly wasn't too far away and offered no resistance to being caught, so Pip and I were soon back home and Molly, safely in the back garden, busily tucked into her feed. After breakfast we all set to work on Molly. Michael didn't always show a tremendous interest in our activities with Molly, but today he was wholeheartedly involved. We brushed and polished the shining dark summer coat and the silky mane and tail. We carefully sponged her eyes, nose and dock; picked out her feet and oiled them with hoof oil on an old paint brush. For once there wasn't much bickering amongst us – no one had time or energy for that – all were intent on the important job in hand. We finished at last and stood back to survey our handiwork. We were all quite sure that Molly would be by far the most beautiful pony at the show, and she would be properly turned out, too!

Although Molly was sparkling clean, we, of course, were filthy. So we left her tied up to the fence and went indoors to wash and change – we must not let her down by being scruffy ourselves.

It was about mid-morning when we eventually set off; three of us, looking, for once, reasonably smart, Molly, looking very dazzling, and two bicycles. It wasn't very far to the show ground, about four miles, I suppose. We took it in turns to ride Molly and the bikes and arrived there about lunch time. It was the first time we had taken our own pony to a show – we had been to shows once or twice with the Riding School but there had always been someone with us to show us what to do – and it was all rather confusing at first. Mike took charge and found a good shady place along the picket lines for Molly. Pip and I stayed with her, away from the bustle and excitement of the show ring, while he went off to find the Secretary's tent, collect our numbers and buy a programme. The programme was most important – we were all dying to see our names in print, especially that of Molly!

By the time Mike returned to us we were well installed under the trees. The sun was hot now and we were glad of the shade. We had taken Molly's tack off and tied her up to the picketing line with her headcollar and rope, which she had been wearing over her bridle during the hack. She seemed quite content to stand and snooze and was apparently unconcerned by all the activity around her.

We pored over the programme eagerly.

'What class is in the ring now?' Pip asked.

'It's the Open Jumping just starting now' Mike said. 'I saw them walking the course when I was over at the Secretary's tent. Then after that there's the Junior Jumping and after that the Gymkhana classes. The showing classes were all judged this morning, of course.'

'Look, look' I shrieked, having grabbed the programme while no one was looking. 'Here we are! Mike's in the potato race, I'm in the bending and then Pip's in the musical poles at the end.'

'For heaven's sake stop shouting.' Mike said, squashingly. 'Everyone will think you've never been to a show before.'

'We've got ages and ages to wait' sighed Pip, 'and I'm terribly hungry. Do you think Mummy and Daddy have arrived yet with the lunch?'

'I expect they're over by the ringside somewhere, watching the jumping. Everyone else has had lunch I'm sure. Do you think Moll will be O.K. if we leave her and go over to the ring?'

We all agreed that Molly looked as if she would be quite happy to sleep for an hour or so, and we made our way to the ringside, with many anxious backward glances. I found a good spot by the ropes where I could see the jumping and also see Molly and get to her quickly if anything happened to upset her, and the others went off in search of our parents. It wasn't long before they all came round to where I was sitting on the grass and we had a super picnic lunch while we watched the jumping. It was terribly exciting to watch and I felt sure that if only we were all better riders Molly could go in and beat them all. It didn't really occur to me that she was only 13.2 h.h. and therefore rather small for an Open Jumping competition. I had utter faith in her ability to outshine all other horses.

When the Junior Jumping had got under way we went back to Molly, who was still standing peacefully where we had tied her, and gave her another rub over with a stable rubber. Then we put her tack on again, and, as Mike's event was first, he mounted and started walking her round to limber her up in good time for the Gymkhana.

I will not bore you with long descriptions of the Gymkhana.

I suppose that in comparison with most shows one goes to today this was a very small show, but you must remember that this was 1948 and the war had not been over long. People were only just beginning to get back to normal and very few people, comparatively, were able to keep horses for pleasure. Show Jumping, as a sport, was still in its infancy, and most shows only included a couple of classes for adults and one for children, and then held their Gymkhana events afterwards, in the main ring. It was a glorious day, there was a good crowd, and everyone was happy to be there looking at pleasure horses once more, or competing with each other for the coveted rosettes.

Mike got really quite keyed up before his class and Molly changed character completely when she was in the collecting ring. She became quite excited and dashing, but he kept her well in hand. He did well in his event, getting into the semi-finals, but did not win a prize. After his event there was an Open Potato race, which took some time, so Molly was able to have a rest before I got on her to prepare for the Bending. I was surprised to find her rather difficult to control in the collecting ring and was afraid I wouldn't manage her in the competition. I had the most simply awful feeling in the pit of my stomach, which was then new to me but is known as 'the needle'. I thought I would be sick or something awful, but fortunately the moment I entered the ring with the three other competitors in my heat the sensation disappeared and I concentrated on the job in hand. Molly was marvellous. She stood like a rock in line at the start and I swear she listened for the word 'go' because she was off like a rocket, in and out the poles, whisked round the end pole and cantered gaily back to the starting line, well ahead of the others. I was overcome with joy and flung my arms round her neck.

'Clever girl, oh clever Molly! – you certainly know your job!' I whispered to her as we left the ring.

However, it wasn't over yet. We were into the semi-final but there was a long way still to go. Molly seemed to know quite well what was expected of her and, although the competitors in the semi-final were much tougher opposition than we had encountered in our heat, she managed to keep her nose in front and we were through to the final. The four of us lined up opposite our poles, and it was a very tense moment. Each time I had come out of the ring into the collecting ring the family had all gathered round Molly and I knew they all hoped I would manage to win something for her. Molly certainly did her best, but our lack of experience now became obvious and we came in last in the final. But we had won a rosette and I was wildly excited. We were called into the ring to collect our ribbons and my excitement passed to Molly. She took hold of the bit in her teeth and charged into the ring. I tugged at her desperately, turned her to one side and expected her to stop as she came up to the ropes round the ring with a row of people seated on the grass just behind them; but she rushed on, leapt over the ropes, people and all, and dashed off across the field! Fortunately I was soon able to regain control and once again we went into the ring, a little more sedately this time, to collect our much treasured white rosette.

There was quite a long wait now, before Pip's turn, and after all her efforts in the bending we felt Molly deserved a short drink. She seemed grateful for the drink, but not at all tired, and once again put up a fine performance in the Musical Poles, but didn't manage to win another rosette.

It was a very happy, tired little band of children, pony and bicycles, who hacked quietly back to Port Meadow, gave Molly her evening feed on the dew-drenched grass, and then went home in the gathering dusk. The white rosette was hung on the wall in the dining room just before supper with much pride by all!

A Jibber – And the Meadow Drive   5

It is one of the more unpleasant, but nevertheless undeniable facts of life, that 'to those who have much, much shall be given'. If you have no pony at all then no-one will consider lending you a pony, even for a day; no-one asks you to look after their ponies whilst they go on holiday, and certainly no-one asks you to school or re-school a pony for them, however competent you maybe. But once you have one pony, then it seems quite easy to acquire others; they just sort of 'happen'.

Although Pip and I were extremely happy to have Molly and had great fun with her, we were very pleased when people asked us if we could ride their ponies for them as it meant we could ride together instead of always having to take turns. One such pony was The Witch, who was lent to us in the Christmas holidays. She was a fat little grey Welsh Mountain pony, about 13.0 hands; and she was a jibber. She would be going along quite sweetly and then, suddenly, without giving you the slightest warning, she would stop. There was no telling how long she would remain standing rigid and immovable, it might be only a matter of 30 seconds or so, but much more often it was 15 or 20 minutes or even longer. There didn't seem to be any reason at all for this jibbing and it certainly was a most annoying habit in a four year old, who was otherwise a very good child's pony. The Witch's owner either didn't have the time or didn't have the inclination to do anything about breaking the habit and re-schooling the pony, and she was lent to us on a more or less permanent basis to ride whenever we wanted.

We persevered with her for many apparently fruitless months, patiently sitting on her when she stopped and simply waiting for her to go on again, which she always did eventually. We thought at first that we were safe enough riding her with Molly because she would surely go with the other pony, but strangely enough this turned out not to be the case, and if the mood came over her she would stop just the same whether Molly was there or not. After months and months of quietly riding The Witch about the Meadow (bareback of course) and being very gentle and patient with her, we began to realize that not only was she stopping much less frequently, but she was remaining still for much shorter periods of time – we were winning!

We tried to buy The Witch (whose real name was Starlight) but her owner wanted too much money for us to pay for her and refused to come to an agreement over price, so we just continued having the use of her, free of charge, which was very nice, without any of the expenses!

Port Meadow was generally at least half flooded in November and only the Wolvercote end, which was much higher ground, remained above water during the winter. We usually came on to the Meadow at the flooded end and cycled along to the end of the raised concrete track used by people with allotments and by the city garbage lorries on their way to the rubbish dump. We left our bikes on the grassy bank, above water level, and then set off along the path towards the nearest dry land! It was a strange sensation. There was water all around us but the path was just high enough to allow us to walk along it without the water going into our wellington boots! On either side of the gravel path was a ditch, so if we went off course at all we were liable to get extremely wet.

37

Once we had caught the ponies, we played marvellous games on them wading through the deep water out to The Mound – a funny round hillock that rose majestically above the lapping waters about 200 yards from the path; or experimenting to see how far we could get on certain of our summer paths that were now under water. We taught both Molly and The Witch to carry one of us along the flooded part of the path to the end of the raised concrete track, and then, when that one had dismounted, to return along the same path, reins carefully knotted up out of the way, to collect the other child who was waiting to scramble aboard and be transported, dry-shod, to the safety of the road and the bikes.

We loved watching the ponies when we let them go in the evenings. There were often the most glorious and spectacular sunsets reflected in the floodwaters on the Meadow, and with the evening clouds banking high and dark in the eastern sky and the paling colours stretching overhead down to the dying sun low on the horizon, the black shapes of the loosed ponies would splash and leap through the waters as they cantered back to their herds, manes and tails streaming in the evening breeze, and the spray from the water lifting and sparkling in the dying rays of the sun. It is hard to think of anything in the world more beautiful than horses in motion.

Once the Christmas holidays were over, riding became more or less impossible during the week, because it was dark so early. However, we didn't go back to school until nearly mid-January and although we grumbled a lot about only being able to see the ponies at week-ends, the time really passed quite quickly and Saturdays and Sundays were more precious to us just because we didn't see Molly during the week. Hay was put out for the animals on the Meadow every day during the winter months and at week-ends we took Molly and The Witch a small supplementary feed.

Often, in January, the flooded part of the Meadow would

freeze over, and then this usually deserted place would be alive with skaters. During the two or three week-ends that the Meadow was frozen we didn't ride much but, after walking the length of the Meadow to find the ponies, see that they were well and happy and give them their feeds, we returned to the scene of the 'winter sports' and joined the happy crowd on the ice.

Neither of us could skate and as none of our friends seemed to have feet the same size as ours we couldn't borrow skates to have a try, so we contented ourselves running and sliding on the ice, and taking long excursions out towards the edge of the river. It was very seldom frozen right across. Usually there was a part right out in the middle of the river where the water still flowed, and we were careful never to go beyond the banks in case the ice wasn't strong enough to hold our weight over the deeper water, but it was fun to be able to visit the boathouses, and the boat hiring stations that were the scene of such activity in the summer and were now forlornly iced in and apparently hibernating. We could run and slide on the ice right past them and on to the very furthest part of the Meadow, the part nearest Oxford, which had once, long ago, been used as a rubbish dump, but now the long-forgotten refuse was covered with earth and grass. This extremity of the Meadow was raised high above the floodwater, and we called the area 'The Bumps' because that was exactly what it was like – a series of bumps! It was possible to drive a car from the road across the Bumps to the boat stations, but not many people bothered to bring cars on to the Meadow. Even so, in summertime it was a rather populated part and so we avoided it most of the time, saving our enjoyment of it for the winter months when there was no-one else there!

Spring was on the way and soon the ice melted and the waters gradually receded and left lush, rich grass for the cattle and horses to gorge themselves on during the lengthening days. Every spring, the Sheriff of the City of Oxford held a Meadow Drive during which all the animals on Port Meadow were driven up to Wolvercote and empounded there until claimed by their owners. If the owner was a commoner of the village of Wolvercote or had rented grazing rights on the Meadow from a commoner, he simply showed these rights to the person at the gate of the pound, claimed his animals, and returned them to the Meadow. But very often the animals belonged to people who were grazing them on the Meadow illegally, and in these cases the owner was fined two guineas for each animal when he claimed it, and he could not return it to the Meadow. The drive took place very early in the morning and although we had often heard about it, we had never actually seen it, so we were wildly excited when we were asked by the owner of the Wolvercote Riding School if we would like to take part!

The greatest secrecy was always maintained before a drive, and those taking part were only informed very late the night before, so that they couldn't remove their animals from the Meadow beforehand. Whilst the drive was on, of course, all the Meadow gates were padlocked and there were a lot of policemen about to see that no one lifted any gates off their hinges!

On the morning of the drive we got up before it was properly light, and went down to the Meadow to catch the ponies. The drive was to start at 6.30 a.m. and everyone was to meet on the Bumps. We found the ponies, who were a little surprised to see us so early in the day, and rode down to the Bumps, Pip on Molly and myself on The Witch. Father was there, complete with camera, and soon other riders began to appear out of the mist. There was quite a big group of riders there when the Sheriff arrived with some Aldermen in a Land Rover. The man in charge of organizing the drive was Randall Wise, who was an old man then but a remarkable character who had, at one time, been a Canadian Mountie, and who still trained horses and gave displays of Western riding and roping at local Horse Shows. Now he approached the Sheriff and asked permission to start the drive.

40

The drive

'I want to take the cattle in first,' he said to us. 'And gently, remember. No one is to go out of a walk. You can have your fun later with the horses but we'll have no "wild west" stuff with these cattle. If you all line up and spread out across the whole width of the Meadow, we can walk quietly up to Wolvercote and as we approach the big double gates there the two extreme ends of our line will move in towards the centre so that we funnel the cattle through the gateway. Just let the horses slip through and stay out here for the time being – but don't leave any cattle behind. You'll find they drive very easily if you take them gently, they just follow each other.'

We all strung out in a long line across the breadth of the Meadow and started walking forward slowly. Randall Wise on his magnificent Grey horse was out ahead of us in the centre of the line. The Witch had never been ridden in so much company before and was very excited and difficult to control. I glanced to my right along the line and spotted Pip on Molly behaving beautifully and looking as if they had been driving meadows for years. Father was busy taking photographs and we must have made a very impressive picture moving slowly across the meadow in the growing light with the mist rising off the damp ground and the first long rays of sunlight catching in the tossing manes of the horses.

Driving the cattle was not, actually, terribly exciting. Just as Randall Wise had said, they walked and jogged meekly in front of us towards the Wolvercote gate, and only once or twice was there a moment of excitement when one tried to break back through the line, to be immediately turned and driven forward again with shouts and threats by the rider nearest. When all the cattle had been safely herded through the gate, three or four riders who did not particularly want to participate in the horse drive took them on down the road to the pound, and the rest of us jogged quietly back up the Meadow to the Bumps.

'Now I'll leave it all to you,' Randall Wise told the bunch of riders. 'But try not to gallop them about too much; we don't want a lot of irate owners when they see their sweated horses.'

I understood now why everyone who had horses on the Meadow legitimately tried to remove them before the drive if at all possible. It was very difficult to drive the horses without galloping them, because they are not placid animals like cattle and they simply *will* gallop, so you have to gallop after them. It's all enormous fun and very spectacular, but the horses being driven are often injured and always frightened and I certainly wouldn't want horses of mine in the drive. Pip and I had great fun helping herd the horses towards the gate. All the drivers stuck together and took the horses in a herd at a time, because it took lots more people, much closer together, to drive the horses successfully than it did to drive the cattle. Molly and The Witch were both good at turning and stopping quickly and we felt they were quite an asset to the whole operation.

Finally the last group of horses was herded down the road to the pound. The morning was well advanced now and we were as hot and tired as our ponies. We watched the steaming, milling horses for a while as they rushed about in the unaccustomed confinement of the fenced in pound, and then we set off at a gentle walk back across the meadow, towards home and lunch. When the ponies were really cool we took them in the river for a drink, watching the glistening drops of water trapped in their whiskers when they raised their grateful muzzles for a breather, and then lowered them again, burying their noses deep in the cool freshness of the river.

Next day we were excited to see pictures of the drive in the local paper and read the brief account. We couldn't help thinking gloatingly of all our friends who would have liked to have been in on the drive but couldn't be, and we rested our ponies and gave them an extra titbit and told them how clever and how famous they were!

Pony Club Camp 6

During the Easter holidays we took Molly to our first Pony Club Rally. We knew hardly anyone in the Pony Club at that time but we were keen to meet other pony owners and to receive more instruction. We hacked the four miles over to the Rally in our customary fashion with Molly and the bicycle to share between us, but when we joined our ride with Molly (we intended to take it in turns to ride her) we were told that she was lame and we should take her home! Now Molly had, in her younger days, done some pony racing and had had an accident which had left her with a slight, but unfortunately just noticeable, peculiarity of the gait at trot. She was not, in fact, lame, but to anyone who didn't know her history she must have appeared so, and the only thing for us to do was to leave the Rally and trail ignominiously home again, very disconsolate and rather bitter at the thought that anyone could believe we would ride Molly if she were lame. Our parents soothed us down that evening and promised to have the vet look at Molly to see if there was anything that could be done.

The vet, when he came, proved to be a tall, well built Scotsman; very kind and very patient with all our questions and with Molly. He told us that at some time in the past she had injured a shoulder muscle and it had never healed properly but that it certainly did not cause her any pain now. He said he would try to do something about the peculiarity of her gait but that the chances of success were slight since it had now become a habit with her to trot the way she did. He explained that he would 'blister' her shoulder in order to try to heal the muscle, and that it would be necessary to keep Molly in a stable for a few days so that she would not move around too much and would rest the shoulder whilst the blister was working.

We had no stable, of course, and didn't really know how to go about finding one, until we suddenly remembered Mr. Hutt, the Greengrocer. Mr. Hutt had a horse and cart and came round twice a week selling fresh fruit and vegetables from door to door. He kept his horse, Daisy, on some water meadows just the other side of the canal, less than a quarter of a mile from our house, and we had sometimes visited her, before we had Molly to occupy all our spare time. Pip thought she remembered some farm buildings in one of the fields, so we decided to ask Mr. Hutt if we could rent a stable from him for a week or so. Mr. Hutt proved to be most accommodating and when we asked him he said that we certainly could rent a stable from him and he also offered to let us turn Molly out in his fields with Daisy for a few weeks after her 'blister' so that she might keep quiet and not run about too much with the other horses on the Meadow. We thanked him profusely and thought how lucky we were to have such kind neighbours, and dashed off down the lane to Daisy's field to inspect the stable and see what was needed to make it ready for Molly's visit.

The stable was actually rather disappointing. It was a partitioned off section of a very old wooden shed, and it was rather dark because it didn't have a proper stable door with a top half that opened, but only a shed door. There was one small window high up on the end wall but no other access for light and air except the cracks between the planks which made up the walls. We were afraid that some of these gaps might cause draughts so we blocked most of them with straw or old sacks. Altogether, we were quite glad Molly would only have to spend

45

a day or two in this stable. We cleaned it out thoroughly and
put down a deep fresh bed of straw, made certain that there
were a couple of good buckets in the shed and plenty of good
hay, and then we went home to telephone the vet, and ask if he
could come the next day to 'blister' Molly.

We caught Molly fairly early the next day and brought her
into the stable and then returned to the house to wait for the
vet. When he arrived we all went down to the stable again to
watch while he rubbed the 'blister' on Molly's shoulder. It
looked just like a black ointment and didn't smell too good.
However, Molly put up with it in her usual stoic fashion and
later on, when it began to burn deep down and must have been
rather painful, she, as always, never made a murmur of
complaint.

It was fun having Molly in the stable and the pleasure of
looking after her was only slightly dimmed by the fact that she
was there to undergo medical treatment. Never has a pony had
such devoted and loving care – we could hardly drag ourselves
away in order to return to the house for meals. But after a few
days in the stable and weeks of rest turned out with Daisy, and
despite all our devoted care, the 'blister' didn't really have
much effect on Molly's trot. The vet advised us not to worry
about it as it certainly didn't cause her any inconvenience now,
but just to carry on using her gently as we had been doing and,
in view of the reception we were likely to get from the Pony
Club, he advised us not to take her to any more Pony Club
activities.

We followed the vet's advice, and occasionally went to
Rallies on The Witch, but we spent most of our time riding on
Port Meadow or in the country round about us at the
Wolvercote and Wytham end of the Meadow. There was,
however, one particular Pony Club activity which I desperately
wanted to attend, and that was the summer Camp. The Pony
Club we belonged to wouldn't take anyone to camp who was
under 13 years of age, but as my 13th birthday was to fall

actually during the week of the camp and since two of my cousins would be there, one as cook and the other as an ordinary member, I was given permission to attend.

The excitement and activity preceding Camp was tremendous. I think Pip was a little disappointed that she could not go, but she cheered up no end when I pointed out to her that she would have Molly all to herself for a whole week whilst I was away, and after that she almost began to feel sorry for me! It had been arranged with The Witch's owners that I should take her to camp; she was, by then, vastly improved and hardly ever jibbed at all, but we felt it would be a wonderful education for her anyway. This was to be my first experience of staying away from my home and family for any length of time and also my first experience of camping, and I must admit that as the date of departure drew nearer I was just a little apprehensive.

The Camp was being held at Letcombe Regis, which is a lovely little village on the edge of the Berkshire downs, and everyone who lived in our area of Oxford was to hack over together on the Wednesday with Pat, the proprietress of a riding school just west of Oxford and a Pony Club Instructor, acting as our guide. It was 23 miles to the Camp and we all assembled in Pat's yard early in the morning, our ponies wearing headcollars over their bridles and mackintoshes tied in awkward bundles in front of their saddles. Anxious parents were fussing backwards and forwards making sure that all the equipment for their particular child had been stowed safely into the wagon which was carrying all the luggage, and giving unheeded last minute instructions to their various offspring about 'not staying in wet clothes' and 'making sure to clean your teeth every night'! It was the middle of August and The Witch was terribly fat. We nearly always rode bareback and I was already worried about the borrowed saddle she had on, and the possibility of girth galls on such a long hack.

We were a very gay cavalcade as we clattered out of the yard and set off across country. It was a glorious day and Pat was very good at avoiding all the roads. She seemed to know the country very well and took us along the headlands of fields as yet unharvested and through deep, thick, green woods. It was soon hot and the flies gathered thickly round the horses' heads so we were glad to stop at mid-morning on the edge of a huge field where there was a cool breeze, and have a drink of lemonade, which was thoughtfully provided by one of the parents who arrived, seemingly from nowhere, in a Land Rover. After about 14 miles, we stopped at a little country pub for lunch. Everything had been laid on in advance and there were good facilities for the ponies, who had certainly earned their rest and feed, as well as for the riders.

The second part of the journey seemed to take much longer than the first, although it was a shorter distance. Perhaps Pat was less sure of the country or perhaps it was just that we were all getting tired now, and so were the ponies. It had clouded over and the day was sultry and thundery with a threat of rain. It was nearly dark by the time we rode into the field where the camp organizers had already put up all the tents and the horse lines. We all found our allocated place in the horse lines – which were large stalls, divided by straw bales with stakes driven through them and into the ground, and with planks and two ropes along the front – took the tack off our tired ponies, rubbed their backs and brushed them off and watered them before giving them their feeds and hay for the night. I was horrified to find that the unaccustomed girth had injured poor Witch quite badly and she now had two large girth galls. I washed them gently with cotton wool soaked in warm water and then went to tell Pat, who was in charge of the horses in camp. She came and inspected the damage and, after washing the raw places again, this time with some cooking salt in the warm water as a disinfectant, she dressed them with Acriflavine and said that I must certainly not put a saddle on the pony again until the galls had completely healed, which would probably take the entire week! Actually, I didn't mind this at all as I was much more used to riding bareback and was somewhat saddle sore myself!

It had started to rain by the time we went to the big marquee for supper and afterwards the four of us in my tent went straight to bed. It was a very small tent and with four sleeping bags spread out on the groundsheet there wasn't any room for anything else, but somehow we all fitted in. My cousin, Frances, was one of my companions in the tent, which was comforting, because I hardly knew the other two girls at all. With much chattering and giggling we settled down for the night, and as soon as there was a lull in the talking I fell fast asleep.

It rained quite hard in the night but by morning it was dry and sunny again. We discovered, when we awoke, that our tent leaked and everything, including most of the sleeping bags and our clothes, were pretty wet. I got up, felt extremely odd, and just managed to disappear behind a bush in time to be very sick. I had been sleeping with my head downhill and that, coupled with all the excitement and the exhaustion of the previous day had finished me off. There was quite a hoo-haa when the people in charge of the camp learnt that we were all wet and that I had been sick, and everything was taken out of the tent to dry in the sun. I was sent to rest in someone's camp bed for the morning, but after a bit I felt fine so I got up and watched some of the instructional rides and groomed The Witch, whom Frances had kindly fed and mucked out for me. I looked at her girth galls and saw that they were rather swollen so I spent some time doing hot fomentations to reduce the swelling before patting the raw patches dry with cotton wool and applying some more Acriflavine.

After lunch everyone went for a hack on the downs but I had to stay in camp with my cook cousin Rosemary. I took The Witch out of the picket lines and lay down on the grass in the shade of some chestnut trees whilst she grazed beside me, which she loved, greedy pony that she was!

49

By the next day everyone had to agree that I had completely recovered. Things had really settled down by now and camp got under way in earnest. I joined in all the activities of the week, without a saddle, even taking part in two small local gymkhanas. Some people thought I was a bit peculiar, riding without a saddle, but that didn't trouble me, and The Witch and I were both much more comfortable that way.

Each morning we were woken up at 7 o'clock and, hastily pulling on jeans and old jerseys and rubber boots, we scrambled out of our tents and ran down to the horse lines. The first thing to do was to give our horses a small net of hay and half a bucket of water, which would keep them busy whilst we did the mucking out. Then we had to wash out the water bucket, refill it with fresh water, and, last of all, give our ponies their grain feed. We left them happily munching and dashed back to our tents to wash our hands and comb our hair and get to the marquee for breakfast at 8. Rosemary was a good cook and after all that hard work we were ravenous, so no-one wanted to be late for meals.

After breakfast we went straight back to the horse lines and groomed our ponies thoroughly, and then returned to our tents to change into riding clothes and tidy our tents before 'Skip', the scout master in charge of camp, came round to inspect. The first ride of the day started at 10 o'clock, so as soon as we had changed, we saddled up (or, in my case, bridled up!) and then went to the arena allocated to the class we were in and lined up for yet another inspection – this time of our tack, our horses and ourselves, by our instructor. All this inspecting sounds terrible, but actually it was probably necessary and it did ensure that we were thorough in our grooming and our tack cleaning.

The instructional rides were interesting and somewhat competitive, particularly when it got to the jumping stages. The jumps were very low, but sometimes we had little competitions round a course of fences incorporating several turns and

50

changes of direction, which demanded more skill than jumping one simple fence, and, of course, we all wanted to do better than our friends in the class. The Witch was a pretty good jumper and seemed to enjoy bouncing down the jumping lane or sailing over the sheep hurdles, which made life fun for me. Some of my friends had ponies who were not nearly so obliging and spent most of their time refusing really little fences. However, gradually we all learnt more about how to cope with unwilling ponies, and how to continue schooling the more obliging ones.

We rode for about an hour and a half and then took our ponies back to their picket lines. We took off the tack and rubbed the sweaty saddle patches dry, gave the ponies a drink and then a small feed, and left them with a small haynet to keep them occupied during our lunch time. The marquee was hot and stuffy and there seemed to be thousands of flies everywhere, so whenever possible we ate our meals at long tables set up in the shade outside, which is by far the best way to eat a camp meal.

After lunch we were all supposed to rest for a while. Being the youngest in camp, I was supposed to lie on my bed, but I usually managed to slip off with my cousin and our tentmates down into the village, where we wandered in the narrow, sun-baked streets, and bought pop and sweets and post cards in the village post office and shop.

On two or three days we had a lecture directly after lunch, which meant we had to stay still and relax for a while. The lectures were all about subjects which interested us tremendously, and most of the lecturers were interesting people, so it wasn't a bit like school. The local vet came along one day and talked about 'Make and Shape of a Pony' and on another occasion a blacksmith came to talk about 'The Foot and Shoeing'.

The afternoon riding session, from around 3.15 to 4.30 was sometimes a hack up on the Downs, with the wind rushing past

51

our ears and blowing our ponies' manes; and sometimes gymkhana games played in the teaching arenas, usually in teams or rides. The afternoon always went very quickly, and at 4.45 we brushed off our ponies, took the droppings out of the stalls, and bedded them down for the night. Once again we filled our water buckets and haynets, this time stuffing them full because this feed had to last all night. Then we all got together in the tack tents, ostensibly to clean our tack but in fact I think more tack got messed up than cleaned in our wild water fights and insane squabbles over which bar of saddle soap belonged to whom. We gave the ponies their last small grain feed at 5.45 and then dashed back to our tents for a quick wash before supper at 6.30. We were supposed to change into clean jeans or a dress for supper, so, as always, it was a mad rush to get to the marquee on time. After supper 'Skip' usually started a camp fire, and we all sat round it and told stories or sang songs or played games in the firelight until bed time. Just before going to bed I always slipped away down to the horse lines to see that all was well with The Witch and refill her water bucket and say good night!

On the Sunday in the middle of Camp week there was an Open Day and parents were invited to Camp. My parents came, of course, riding their tandem, with Pip on her little Fairy-cycle beside them. It was a marathon ride for an 11 year old, 20 miles there and the same distance home again in the evening, but we were used to going long distances by bicycle because, although we did, in fact, have a car, petrol was rationed and the car could only be used for essential journeys. The roads were a good deal safer and more pleasant then!

I was thrilled to be able to show my family how much The Witch and I had improved as they watched my ride perform in the teaching arena; and then, in the evening we all sat together by the camp fire, and listened to a talk given by the local Huntsman, who simply delighted everyone by blowing his hunting horn and teaching us all the different calls.

52

When camp broke up on Wednesday morning, we all felt that we had learned a lot, that our riding had improved and that our ponies were better behaved. We had made so many new friends and had had so much fun together that the long hack home was rather silent and sad as we all thought how we should miss each other. My saddle was sent home in the truck and I hacked The Witch bareback so that I would not re-open her girth galls, which had now healed up well.

When we reached Pat's yard once more, and the time had come to part from our new friends, we called our good-byes to each other together with promises to 'write soon' which were, of course, never fulfilled, and I set off back to the Meadow, happy and tired, with a tired, but much better mannered little grey pony.

The Hunter Trials   7

As soon as I got home from Camp, Pip showed me a schedule
which had arrived for some Hunter Trials to be held in
September on Boar's Hill, which is a rather exclusive
residential area about four miles from the city centre.

'Let's take Molly' she said excitedly. 'The Darbys are
organising it, and look, the classes are arranged into just the
right age groups for us, so we could all have a go.'

It seemed a splendid idea. The Darbys had a small riding
school on Boar's Hill and we knew them well. The cousins I had
been with at Camp lived on the Hill, too, in a rambling old
bungalow with three acres of fascinating, overgrown garden.

'We could hack the five miles or so across country from the
Meadow to Polstead,' I said, catching Pip's enthusiasm, 'rest
there, or perhaps even leave Molly with Fra for the night before
the Trials, and hack the last half mile on the morning of the
show.'

We studied the schedule carefully, and with mounting
excitement. It certainly was conveniently arranged from our
point of view. There was a class for children 12 years and
under, ponies not to exceed 13.2 h.h., which would be splendid
for Pip on Molly as she was only 11 and Molly was just 13.2
h.h. Then there was a class for children 14 years and under,
ponies not to exceed 14.2 h.h. in which I could compete on

Molly. There was also a class for children 16 years and under, horses any height, and we thought Mike could take her in that class if he didn't mind being slightly undermounted. Mike had had his 16th birthday in April and when he had arrived home from school for the summer holidays we had scarcely recognized him, he had shot up so much! When we talked to him about it, Mike seemed just as keen on the idea of the Hunter Trials as we were, but he pointed out that he would look ridiculous on Molly now he was so tall, and after much discussion, he decided to hire a horse for the day from another riding school on the Hill and compete on that.

In great excitement we made out our entries and sent them off, and then, because we had only ever seen horse shows and gymkhanas in the past, we spent the next week wondering what to expect at Hunter Trials. We didn't particularly want to show our ignorance, however, so Pip and I decided to question our cousins cunningly the following Sunday, when, as usual, we would be going to Polstead for tea. Frances had also received a schedule and was planning to go in the same class as Mike, so it wasn't at all hard to get her to talk about Hunter Trials in general, and the coming event in particular.

'I don't expect the course will be very big' she mused 'because no-one's hunters will be fit yet. The spring ones are always bigger. And the best thing about Hunter Trials is that they will all be natural fences. Sometimes there's a gate to be opened, to prove how handy your horse is, but not always.'

'How long do you think the course will be?' I asked, a little confused by the picture I now had in my mind of what exactly Hunter Trials were.

'Oh, well, I expect it will vary according to the class' Fra said airily, but I secretly suspected she didn't really know.

As it happened, Frances was absolutely right and the course did vary in length a little, being shorter for Pip's class and having quite a big extra loop for the 16 and under. We had hacked Molly up to Polstead fairly early on the morning of the great day, and eaten an early lunch there before going on to the Hunter Trials with Fra and Mike, who had joined us at Polstead with a good looking grey horse he had hired for the day. We left the horses tied up and went to get our numbers from the Secretary's tent, and here we discovered carefully drawn plans of the courses displayed on boards outside, which Pip and I studied intently for some time.

'Aren't you going to walk the course?' Fra appeared suddenly behind us. 'Come on, you've loads of time, we could all go round together.'

It was a most encouraging looking course, at the start, anyway. The first fence was a small brush, not more than 2 ft. 3 ins. high and quite close in front of the Secretary's tent. Then the course went on across the field, over a post and rails, which looked enormous (but Fra said they would take the top rail off for our classes), and then into a little wood. It was quite easy to follow the course because there were yellow arrows nailed to trees or stuck on stakes between the fences to show the direction, and the fences were each marked with a number. Number three was a little pile of logs in the path through the woods and this was followed by a ditch, which didn't look much, but which Fra said would cause a lot of trouble to some people because lots of ponies don't like ditches. Then we turned right and the next fence was a low stone wall leading into a muddy farmyard which we had to cross and jump out of over a post and rails.

Here the course for the two younger age groups turned left and went on over some straw bales, but there was a loop added for Frances's and Mike's class, so we decided to walk round this loop too, since we had heaps of time. They had to continue over a hedge into the next field and go right out into this field, down a dip and over a log into a muddy pond, across the pond, and out again over a low rail, and then curve back left handed over a bullfinch. I hadn't seen a bullfinch before and it looked huge and thick. Fra explained that only the bottom 3 ft. of it was solid hedge, all the rest – and there was lots more, I suppose it was over 5ft. high in all – was just flimsy twigs and you jumped *through* them.

This brought the seniors back onto the original course and they turned right and continued over a low rail with quite a drop into a lane, which we would also have to jump as our eighth fence. We turned left in the lane and went along to the end of it, where there was an enormous gate. Fortunately a competitor came along on the course just then and I realized with relief that we had to stop and open the gate, and close it again, but not jump it! Then we found we were back in the field where we had started, but on the far side from the Secretary's tent. The next fence was an Irish bank, which was about 2 ft. 6 ins. high and at least 6 ft. wide, perhaps more. You were supposed to jump up on to it and then jump down the far side, of course, so it didn't look too terrifying. After this there were some sheep hurdles which weren't more than 2ft. 6 ins. and a left turn to a narrow style where we saw several people get refusals later on, as their horses didn't like the narrow fence with its high wings. The last jump of all was a tiger trap, which nearly all horses jump well because of its shape, with a good groundline well out on the take-off side, and after this you galloped straight on through the finish posts, which were very close to the start – to help the timers, Fra said.

We watched a few more competitors round the last bit of the course and noticed that the judges were careful only to have three people on the course at the same time. Whenever someone finished, another competitor was started, and no-one else started until another rider finished! Mike said it was probably to avoid a pile up if someone was having refusals somewhere on the course, and also, they probably only had three stop-watches! It seemed rather a complicated procedure, and we wondered how they decided who had won. Pip said she thought it must be a combination of time and jumping clear, as she had noticed judges at the jumps out of sight of the start, and they must be marking those fences and then sending the results back to the Secretary's tent at the end of the class.

Soon we thought it was time for Pip to get mounted and have a practice jump, so we made our way back to Molly, and found that while we had been walking the course our parents had arrived on the tandem and they were standing talking to Molly, Kanga (Fra's horse) and Mike's grey, keeping them company until we got back.

Because we spent most of our time riding on Port Meadow, which is very flat and doesn't have any natural obstacles, we didn't really get much jumping in our everyday riding. However, we had been practising over fences we had made for ourselves out of piles of driftwood and broken branches during the past few weeks and we hoped Molly had more or less got the idea by now. Molly, of course, must have done quite a lot of jumping when she belonged to the riding school, and we had ridden her in the jumping paddock there before we had bought her.

Pip mounted and rode around the collecting area for a bit and then Mike and I went off with her to find the practice fence and make sure she popped over it a few times to warm up. Molly loved jumping and was pretty good at it, but she was also very rapid! She seemed to think that she could clear any obstacle provided she was going fast enough and she had long since passed the age where she might have been re-schooled to jump a little more slowly. It was no use pulling and tugging at her mouth, because she paid no attention to that at all and you only wore yourself out. In any case, she was far too sensible to land herself in trouble and the best way to ride her was the way Pip rode her, with perfect confidence, just sitting relaxed on her strong back, and not interfering with her at all.

Pip's class had begun, so we moved back to the collecting ring. There seemed to be quite a big entry and several of them looked terribly professional. Molly was rather fat, and her mane was unplaited, but she looked well brushed and her neat

58

Up the hill to the tiger trap

little hooves shone with the oil so recently applied.

At last it was Pip's turn to go and we all stood close to the start, holding our breath and urging her on in our hearts. Molly cantered calmly enough towards the first fence and popped over and then went on towards the post and rails, gathering speed all the time. She sailed over and out of our sight, but Pip told us later that she was simply super through the wood and the farmyard, but a bit hard to turn left for the straw bales, as she thought she should go straight on. However, they had sorted that out and Molly popped over the rail into the lane and we caught sight of her again as she opened and closed the gate back into the field. She stood like a rock whilst Pip fumbled for what seemed ages with the catch, then turned and sped towards the Irish bank. Either Molly had never encountered an Irish bank before, or else she thought this one beneath her dignity, for she gathered herself back on her hocks and gave an enormous leap, clearing the whole thing in one go! Pip, who had been expecting a neat little jump on to the top of the bank, was nearly jumped off, but grabbed a handful of Molly's flying mane and stayed with her, guiding her towards the sheep hurdles. Molly was really galloping on now, but never made a mistake, flew the hurdles and the stile and came on up the hill fast, over the tiger trap and through the finish flags.

Pip slid off her back and we all rushed to congratulate both of them and help her loosen Molly's girths and walk her about till she got her breath back.

'Do you think we went fast enough?' Pip panted anxiously. 'And did you see the way she flew the bank!' How could we possibly have missed it? The whole crowd had roared with laughter, seeing Molly's huge leap, but we thought she was terribly clever and very bold to have jumped so faultlessly over a fence she did not know how else to cope with. She was sweating a bit now, and blowing quite hard, although Pip said she only trotted along the lane, because Molly seemed to be a

60

bit blown then. But there was plenty of time to walk her about and cool her off before my class began.

I have never been able to work out how the judges decide who has won in Hunter Trials – perhaps they are all different, because it never turns out to be the people who seem to have gone round fastest. Of course, without a stop-watch it's impossible to tell who was really fastest and not being able to see the whole course all the time you can't really know who has gone clear. However, despite Pip's speed, when they announced the winners she was not amongst them. If she was disappointed, she didn't show it, she said that she had had such fun going round the course she didn't care who won, and that if she would have had to press Molly faster to win, then she was glad to be out of it, because Molly had gone a good pace and it would not have been fair to ask for even more from such a generous pony!

I knew I didn't really stand any chance of winning anything in my class because many of the ponies would be a hand bigger than Molly and would naturally be able to go faster, so I determined just to enjoy jumping the course and do the best I could to make a good clear round. Soon I heard the loudspeaker calling for my class, so I mounted and took Molly over the practice fence, for my benefit – not hers, since she knew now what was expected of her. Once again, in the collecting ring, I experienced the sick, nervous, feeling that I still have today before a competition. I felt completely weak at the knees and I very nearly turned round and left the collecting ring and withdrew from the competition. Once I was between the starting flags I felt fine – of course.

'Go!' said the starter, dropping his arm and starting his stop-watch, and Molly leapt forward almost taking me by surprise. We flew the brush and the rails and swung round left handed in the wood going much too fast towards the logs. The wind was tearing through my hair – my hat had mysteriously fallen off at the second fence – and I suddenly realized I was tugging on the reins like mad. I stopped pulling at Molly and held some mane.

'Steady, Molly!' I gasped, and surprisingly enough she did steady, jumped the logs, and slowed down almost to a trot before carefully jumping the ditch. She was quite easy to swing around right handed and we sailed over the wall into the farmyard and out again over the rails. Then I had the left turn to make to the straw bales, but Molly wasn't too difficult, although left was her bad side, because she remembered the course, I suppose. We slowed right down for the rail with the drop into the muddy lane, and trotted down the lane to the gate. Now I realized why Pip had seemed to take such ages here, the gate was heavy and the latch difficult. But Molly stood like a statue once more and as soon as I had finished we swung round and headed for the Irish bank. I held my breath, wondering if she would fly it again or bank it. I felt her gather herself, crouch, and spring – a huge leap, right off her hocks, and we were flying through the air to land safely well beyond the bank. She had done it again! The crowd loved her and roared its delight. Molly seemed to have got her second wind now and galloped smoothly on over the hurdles and the style and then the tiger trap, and she finished strongly again up the hill.

I leapt off, breathless and excited. It had been the most exhilarating experience and although Molly and I were both puffing and blowing, we had enjoyed it enormously. Of course, we didn't win anything, but somehow winning seemed to matter much less at a hunter trial than at a horse show. Molly had finished now for the day, and we took off her tack and walked her about until she was completely dry, and then tied her to the fence so that we could all watch Frances and Michael in the next class.

Mike was mounted on the big grey, preparing for his class which had started by then. He jumped the practice jump a couple of times and then joined the crowd in the collecting ring. After what seemed an age he was called to the start, and then he was off. He jumped the first two fences beautifully, and then was lost to view. He said afterwards that his horse went splendidly until he reached the pond, where he had a refusal before he could persuade him to jump into the murky water. Quite soon we saw him at the gate – which he managed much better than either Pip or I had, and we held our breath, wondering how he would cope with the bank. His horse, however, had no intention of playing Pegasus and jumped neatly onto the bank and hopped off again easily before galloping on to complete the course in fine style. We all thought he had done terribly well, so it was disappointing to hear about the refusal at the pond, which would certainly keep him out of the ribbons. However, Frances had yet to go, and we had high hopes of her and Kanga. She did not disappoint us. They made a lovely clear round in very good time and were awarded second prize amidst much clapping and many congratulations from the spectators.

The afternoon had really drawn into evening by now, but fortunately it was summer time and would not be dark until late. Our parents said that Mike must hack Molly home for us after he had returned the grey to the stables up the road, because it was going to be much too late by the time we all got back if the three of us went together through the woods. It was really much easier for us to ride down the road on our bicycles, if I rode Michael's, and for Father to go and meet him at the Meadow with the tandem. So, with a little grumbling about not being allowed to take Molly home, but secretly rather relieved because we were very tired, Pip and I set off for Oxford in close formation with the parents on the tandem, and Mike and Molly swung off across the fields at her brisk walk, leaving a dark trail through the already dew-drenched grass. She must have been tired, but only her natural gaiety showed, and she too, like us, seemed to have thoroughly enjoyed her first attempts at hunter trialing.

Christmas   8

The summer holidays were suddenly over, and when the new school term started I had homework every evening. As the days grew shorter it was only possible for us to see Molly at the week-ends. This did not, of course, disturb Molly, who was well used to a natural life on the meadow and was growing a good thick coat which would keep her warm enough when the winter became severe. So long as a pony has regular food, clean fresh water, and some sort of natural shelter, like a good thick hedge, from the worst of the weather, it will winter out quite happily. I have walked across Port Meadow late on a winter's night, knowing there to be about two hundred head of cattle and horses turned out there, and not found a trace of one of them; because they were all sheltering tight up under the hedges.

As the autumn wore on, Molly seemed to change. She was perfectly healthy and she was certainly not getting thin. In fact, she seemed to be getting fatter! Our house was rather unusual in that the front door and the back door were side by side, with a plank gate at right angles between them, dividing the front garden from the back. It was necessary for Molly to walk through this gateway as she went down the long, narrow passage at the side of the house to the back garden where she spent the lunchtimes at week-ends, and we soon began to speculate on how much longer she was going to be able to get through! Each week-end Molly was made to stand exactly between the gateposts so that we could stand directly behind her and see just how much space there was left between her 'barrel' and the gateposts on each side. As the space diminished, we began to think that she really must be in foal! She was not supposed to be in foal, of course, and at her age it seemed highly improbable, but there was nothing else to account for her changing shape.

The middle of winter is not the usual time for a foal to be born and our parents were, on the whole, disinclined to believe that Molly could really be going to produce one. Nevertheless, it naturally became the main subject of conversation since Molly had already become the true centre of our family, and after many discussions and disagreements Father finally said one day:

'If that mare produces a foal, I will put an announcement in the Oxford Mail.' We weren't quite sure whether this was supposed to be the ultimate proof of his disbelief of the possibility, or a way of tempting the powers that be into working a miracle for us. So far as Pip and I were concerned, by the time the Christmas holidays started there was no longer the slightest doubt that Molly was going to have a foal, and very soon, too – how we hoped and prayed that it would come on Christmas day!

Christmas preparations kept us all busy during the first few days of the school holidays. There were still all the local Christmas cards to write and send off, some last minute presents to buy, and the house to clean and decorate with greenery. Our Christmas tree and the holly we used to decorate the house always came from our cousin's garden at Polstead, so the whole family spent one happy afternoon in the overgrown grounds of our aunt's house, choosing a tree for each household and cutting stacks of scarlet berried holly. By the time we had finished it was already dusk and this added to our excitement as we clambered on to the country bus that would take us back to Oxford with our armfuls of holly and our six foot tall Christmas tree. We never brought the tree into the house until Christmas Eve, so the next morning we planted it securely in a bucket of earth and left it in the garden, safely out of Molly's reach.

Christmas Eve came at last. The air was soft and damp and almost springlike as, very early, Pip and I made our way to the Meadow to see that Molly was all right. We didn't ride that day, but took her a feed and spent some time talking to her and stroking her. It wasn't only that her shape had changed; she seemed to have changed in herself, as well, she was more docile and dreamy – or did we imagine it! Anyway, after re-assuring ourselves that the foal was not likely to arrive that day, we left Molly with a final pat and returned to the house.

There were so many other excitements crowding in on us now that we almost forgot about Molly. We were to be allowed to go to Midnight Mass that night and so we were supposed to have a rest in the afternoon, but Pip and I were much too excited to rest properly and instead we put the final touches to our present wrapping and decorating, stuffing as much dark, shiny holly as possible into the big bedroom we shared. Later on in the afternoon we brought the Christmas tree into the lounge and, after wrapping the bucket round with gay red crepe paper, we set about decorating the tree. Most of our decorations were very old, and many of them a bit broken or tatty, but we loved them all dearly and took them out of the decorations box each year with the added joy of greeting old friends.

There was the beautiful 'Silver Chain' which was very long and made of thin glass tubes and silver balls strung together like a giant necklace – this had been sent by an aunt in Canada and was therefore doubly loved, for its beauty and for reminding us of a favourite aunt! There were some fascinating coloured glass balls, and coloured glass geese with white tail feathers, and small black felt elves stuck onto orange paper leaves. There were glass icicles to be tied carefully on the tips of branches and coloured candles in little holders which were always attached to the tree, but which were never lighted. There were hedgehogs and tiny fairy dolls and smaller chains and just a very little tinsel, and there was a beautiful, if slightly tarnished, Star of Bethlehem which Mike was tall enough to attach to the very top of the tree. When Father came home he arranged the coloured electric lights and dealt with all the intricacies of the wiring, which none of us were allowed to touch, and then came the magic moment we had all been waiting for. We turned out all the lights in the room and Father turned on the coloured lights on the tree. For a moment we gazed spellbound – how beautiful it looked, and almost mysterious, too. The dim light from the tiny coloured bulbs sparkled on the decorations but left deep, strange shadows within the heart of the tree. And then the lights were turned on again and everyone was rushing about fixing the last minute decorations and putting up even more Christmas cards.

By the time we had finished decorating the tree Mother was ready for some help in the kitchen, stuffing the turkey. If it was to be cooked in time for Christmas dinner it had to go into the oven during the night and so it must be prepared before we got dressed for Midnight Mass. We all took turns pushing stuffing inside the big, clammy bird and then helped to sew it up and truss it ready for roasting. The kitchen was warm, and smelled good; of spice and herbs and raw poultry and chestnuts, but there was an open fire in the dining room making warm, inviting patterns on the rug, so I allowed myself to be lured back and sat down on the floor close to the fire. The radio was on and I sat gazing into the fascinating flames, half listening to the story of Rumplestiltskin, half dreaming, tired now, and stifling the yawns which kept on coming, but determined not to give in and doze in case no-one woke me in time for church.

Suddenly it was time to get ready, and with all the rushing

67

about which always accompanied my family's efforts to get ready for church, I woke up again properly. We had to put on really warm clothes as the church was a mile away and we cycled through the frosty air, our bicycle tyres hissing on the damp road, the blackness pierced by the little yellow gleams from our front lamps. We were a splendid cavalcade, with Father and Mother on the tandem, Pip beside them on her small bike, and Michael and I cycling behind on our grown-up machines, gazing up from time to time at the stars and sniffing the midnight air.

We actually arrived at the church about 11.30 p.m. because we knew it would be packed and unless we were there early we would not get a seat. Ours was a little church, very friendly and simple. We always sat in the same pew, two from the front on the right hand side! As we walked up the aisle to take our places Pip and I craned our necks to see over to the left of the altar where Father Carter had built a beautiful crib. He always made it so real looking and each year he changed it slightly. There were the figures of Joseph and Mary and the Shepherds and an ox and a donkey. And streaming down on the empty manger – the figure of the baby Jesus would not be put in the manger until after the Mass – were real rays of light from a star high above the crib!

There is nothing so moving and warming as Midnight Mass at Christmas and we were all happy, singing inside ourselves, repeating over and over again the stirring verses of the 'Adeste Fideles', the final hymn, as we pedalled home, feeling the early morning air, subtly different, rushing past our ears! It was Christmas Day – the baby Jesus was born and lying safe and warm in the crib. I had prayed that God would send Molly a lovely foal, perhaps an irreverent prayer, but certainly one made in complete sincerity and faith. When we arrived home we all had a glass of sherry before going to bed. We raised our glasses and clinked them together wishing each other 'Happy Christmas!'. The sherry made us feel very grown-up, and it also made us very sleepy!

Our house was very much like any other house full of children on Christmas morning. Despite the fact that we knew quite well, and had known for years, that it was our parents who filled our Christmas stockings, we all firmly maintained that we believed in Father Christmas, so we each got a stocking filled with interesting and delicious things suspended at the foot of our beds. There were chocolate mice, humming tops, sweets, nuts and always a tangerine or an apple, most of which we ate on the spot. Our official present opening was always held after breakfast. It was a long drawn out but thrilling time, as everyone watched everyone else open one present at a time, carefully removing the bright Christmas paper, or tearing the wrappings off; depending on the character of the person opening the parcel, and discovering each time some exciting, almost un-hoped-for treasure, within. This took a considerable time and it wasn't until quite late in the morning that Father and Mike and Pip and I went down to the Meadow to find Molly and take her her special Christmas feed, with lots of juicy carrots and apples chopped up in it. We hoped and hoped that the foal would be there, but when we found Molly she was unchanged – very pleased to see us, but still without the foal we dreamed of trotting at her heels.

MIDWAY COUNTY LIBRARY

A New Arrival 9

Pip and I weren't particularly good at stable building, but obviously Molly could not be left on the Meadow if she had a foal and where else could she go but into the garden! So the day after Christmas we started work, and in a couple of days a weird looking loose box, made mostly of willow branches tied together with string, took shape on our tiny patch of lawn. We didn't feel that, even then, the rest of the family was convinced that Molly was going to have a foal, but we were so certain about it that we simply had to get on and improvise a stall as best we could.

At 8.0 o'clock on the morning of January 3rd the telephone rang, and Mother answered it.

'Hello. This is Josie' said a voice at the other end of the line which Mother had immediately recognized as belonging to one of the girl instructors at the Riding School at Wolvercote. 'I think you should go to the Meadow quickly. Molly has had a foal and all the other horses are milling about with excitement, I'm afraid it will get hurt!'

As Mother thanked Josie for calling and put down the 'phone we all rose from the breakfast table with shrieks of excitement. Father was away in Cheltenham on a business trip and he would not be back until later that morning, but we knew something must be done quickly. We were far too excited to

Keeping other horses away

think coherently and leaving a scatter of dirty breakfast dishes in our wake, Mike and Pip and I tore through the house, grabbed our bicycles and rushed off down to Port Meadow.

We found Molly's herd right in the middle of the Meadow, a little nearer to Wolvercote than home. They were certainly excited; all except Molly, that is, for she was apparently unaware that the tiny new foal had anything to do with her and she was calmly grazing some distance away whilst a huge old Percheron mare was licking the foal, and her companion, a Percheron gelding, was keeping the squealing, pounding herd at bay so that they didn't trample on the foal.

After a while the woolly little foal got unsteadily to its feet and staggered towards the Percheron's flank on wobbly legs. Instinct told the foal where to seek the nice warm milk it wanted, but, of course, the Percheron mare had no milk for it. We thought it was time we took a hand in things, so very quietly we caught Molly and took her up close to the foal and then, manhandling it gently, we pushed its nose under Molly's flank. She was a little upset at first, but once the foal had suckled from her she seemed to understand perfectly that it belonged to her and that she must look after it. The other horses were still rushing about and it was obvious that we must get the mare and foal away from them and off the meadow if the baby was to escape being trampled to death. We had dashed out of the house so quickly that we hadn't even thought of bringing a halter with us and we knew we really needed help, so I got on my bike again and pedalled for home as fast as I could, leaving the other two to guard the foal as best they could.

Father was driving back from Cheltenham to Oxford enjoying the crisp, cold day full of bright sunshine and clear blue sky. He arrived at the house, his thoughts set on lunch, just as I was telling Mother all about the foal. I rushed at him almost before he could get through the door.

'Molly has a lovely little filly foal,' I was shouting in my excitement, 'do come and see her, quickly! Pip and Mike are staying with her to look after the foal and all the other horses are round them trying to see it, so we must go straight away and bring them both back here before it gets trampled on!'

'Steady, steady,' Father said, 'Wait a minute. I think the best thing is to ring the Vet and get him to come with us and have a look at them to make sure everything is all right.'

The Vet lived less than a mile away and when Father telephoned he was eating his lunch and obligingly promised to be along in about half an hour. He was the same vet who had blistered Molly's shoulder for us, so we already knew and liked him and had great confidence in him. When he arrived we all set off for the Meadow, taking the vet's car as far as possible and then walking the rest of the way to where I had left Pip and Mike with Molly about an hour before. This time I had taken a bridle along for Molly and an old dog collar and lead which I thought would just about fit the tiny foal.

When we finally reached the herd Pip and Mike were still doing their best to protect Molly and her foal, but it was not an easy assignment, and, in fact, Molly and the Percheron mare were trotting round side by side in big circles and the foal looking smaller than ever beside the cart mare, was sandwiched between them, having to canter as fast as it could to keep up! Meanwhile the other horses were milling about and making a thorough nuisance of themselves.

Between us we managed to catch Molly and the Percheron and then the Vet was able to get hold of the foal. The poor little thing was nearly run off its feet already and although nature designed foals with specially long legs and made them able to run about almost as soon as they are born, they also need lots of time to sleep and rest! The Vet examined the foal and Molly and pronounced them both perfectly fit, but he said that they must be moved from the meadow at once; otherwise the foal might easily be kicked by one of the over-excited horses in the herd, or they might make Molly gallop about so much that the foal could be galloped to death.

Pip and I knew, of course, that we were going to take Molly home and stable her in the garden .This was what we had been preparing for ever since Christmas. Father kept saying things like, 'We have no field' and 'I wonder who would rent us a field at such short notice.' But we kept up an excited cajoling and quite soon he gave in, because there was obviously nothing else to be done for the time being but bring Molly and her daughter home to our back garden! We slipped the dog collar round the foal's tiny, woolly neck and set off towards home. The Percheron mare wanted to come too and we felt mean about shooing her away, but she had had a lot of fun out of the foal already, and soon her friend, the big Percheron gelding, came over to her and they started grazing close up side by side, for company.

We had to laugh as we watched the tiny foal, still full of beans despite all its exertions. It was just the tiniest foal you can imagine, more like a dog than a pony, and with such a small head that it was several weeks before she grew big enough to wear a foal-slip, so she had to continue to wear the dog collar and lead on every outing.

By the time we reached home it was well into the afternoon and although we had this flimsy structure which we called a stable already set up in the garden, we had no straw and no hay. Father and Mike took the tandem and I took my bicycle, and leaving Pip and Mother to watch over Molly, we set off to the local corn merchant's shop. Here we bought two bales of straw and a bale of hay and, much to the amazement of the salesman, we balanced these – and the bags of bran and oats which Father also bought, saying that Molly should have some concentrated protein food to help her to produce enough milk for the foal—on our bicycles, and set off for home, pushing our precarious loads!

When we got home we soon had Molly's stall bedded knee deep in the clean, fresh smelling, wheat straw, which would keep her and the filly warm and comfortable. We had always left Molly tied up when she was in the garden, but we couldn't leave her tied up now, with the foal, in case it got tangled up in the halter rope, so we just let her loose, gave her a big bucket of fresh water and plenty of hay, and trusted her not to push her way through the flimsy sides of her stall. By the time all the bedding down had been finished, and Father and Michael had made one or two improvements to the structure of the stall, it was already dark, so we gave Molly a small feed of damp bran and oats and left her contentedly munching, with her beautiful little daughter curled up fast asleep in the lovely warm straw. Late that night, before he went to bed, Father went quietly outside to make sure that all was well and to fill up Molly's water bucket. He was greeted by a happy little whinny from Molly – she simply couldn't have been more content with life.

The next morning Pip and I were up and out in the garden almost before it was light. It was quite cold, but the air was dry and clear and later on the sun would be warm and bright. We were up early, but not before the foal. As we came down the path we saw her having her first feed of the day. We stood and watched her suckling and laughed at her when she had finished because there were droplets of white milk all over her furry muzzle! We checked that Molly had plenty of milk for her new daughter and then started cleaning out the stable, carefully removing all the droppings and the wet straw and making a neat manure pile as far away as possible from the house, and the stable. Meanwhile the foal was exploring all round the stall and soon found that she could fit quite easily between the improvised bars, so she hopped out into the garden and, suddenly finding green grass under her feet – at that time there was still *some* lawn left – she stuck her little head up in the air and, with curly tail flying, she galloped excitedly up and down the tiny garden, stopping short at the wire fence of the chicken run and snorting at the frightened, clucking hens! Molly moved a little anxiously around the stall, but did not try to follow her daughter through the bars.

When we had finished mucking out, we brushed Molly over quickly with a dandy brush, just to make her feel good, and then gave her fresh water and hay and another small feed of bran and oats. We pushed the foal gently back inside the stall, and ran into the house for breakfast.

From our point of view there was no more ideal arrangement of life than to have Molly and the foal in the garden, but our parents now concerned themselves with the question of finding a field somewhere fairly near by. We couldn't do anything about this problem, so we cheerfully left it to them and spent a glorious day looking after Molly and her baby. After breakfast, we decided that Molly must have some exercise and we also knew that it was bad for her to be without grass, since she was used to getting grass all the time, even if we provided her with plenty of hay. We thought it would be a good idea for the foal to have some more room to run about, too, so we put a halter on Molly and the dog collar on the foal and set off down the road to the nearest part of Port Meadow.

We didn't have to go far along the road because we used the canal towing path for part of the way, and then a cart track which led over a narrow railway bridge and on to the meadow at a side gate – not more than half a mile from home. We spent the whole morning on the Meadow, letting Molly graze all the time, but being careful to stay well away from all the other animals. We kept Molly on the halter in case she got any ideas about rejoining her herd, but she seemed quite content to stay near the gate and eat the long, lush grass. (One of the most wonderful things about Port Meadow is that there is always lush grass growing there, even in winter time, because it is so wet.) The foal was delighted to see wide open spaces again and as soon as we took her collar off she rushed around in big circles at her funny, bouncy little canter. After a bit she made a dash back to Molly, took a long drink, and then suddenly flopped down in the warm sunshine to sleep!

Father was as good as his word and had inserted an announcement in the Oxford Times under the heading Births. 'To Molly Rose of 12 Bainton Road, Oxford, the precious gift of a daughter' we read, avidly, when we had settled Molly for the night and gone into the house for supper to find Father, just home from the office, brandishing several copies of the paper. We were all delighted with this announcement and it had two rather exciting results – one was a large amount of post over the next few days addressed to Molly Rose advertising the advantages of buying a cot, pram, and other baby goods from such and such a shop; and the other was the arrival the very next day of a photographer who took pictures of the new baby with her mother, in the garden. A story and the picture appeared in the Oxford Mail the next day to our huge delight!

At every meal the conversation revolved round the two big questions yet to be solved: where to find a field for Molly and what to call the foal. As the next few days passed and the foal grew stronger and more lively every day, she dashed about the garden so madly that we were afraid she might hurt herself. We took her and Molly to the meadow every morning so that she could run about and Molly could graze, but she naturally spent a good deal of the time there curled up asleep and obviously she needed a field as soon as possible so that she could be really free to run about in safety at all times. One great blessing was the really wonderful way Molly behaved. She never tried to move from her improvised 'stall' and was not the slightest trouble.

It was the foal's liveliness that finally settled the matter of her name. There was almost continual discussion and argument on this point and as fast as one member of the family suggested a name, someone else thought of an objection to it and suggested something else. At last someone said 'She's so fizzy, why don't we call her "Shandy"'. For once we all agreed that the name suited her perfectly, so 'Shandy' she became.

At last Father succeeded in renting an old farmyard with a field

77

and an orchard attached, not far out of Oxford along the Eynsham Road. It was land that had been sold by the farmer just before the war for building and, due to building restrictions and shortage of materials following the war, it was still not built on and would not be used for two or three years anyway. There was a good fresh water supply and plenty of shelter under the thick hedges, a few shade trees, and the old farm buildings which could be used if the weather got really bad although they were in a pretty poor state of repair.

We decided that Molly and Shandy should make the journey to their new home on Saturday. Father would be at work, but Michael was still at home on his Christmas holiday and Mother would be there as well, so there would be four of us and we thought we should be able to accomplish the move successfully. It was only about three miles from our house to the farm by the main roads but we didn't want to take Molly and Shandy through all the crowds and the traffic, so we planned a very roundabout route which, although much longer, kept us to the fields and quieter lanes as much as possible. The last quarter of a mile would have to be along the main Eynsham Road, but by that time we would be far enough from the centre of the town for it not to be too busy. Pip and I hadn't seen the field yet but Father and Mother had cycled over on the tandem, taking Mike along too, and they had carefully checked all the fences and made sure that the stream running through the field was clean and suitable for horses and that there were no death traps in the form of discarded farm implements or broken bottles hidden in the grass or the hedges.

We set off early on Saturday morning, taking it in turns to lead Molly, and Shandy, and push the bicycles (we had to have some transport to get us home). The first part of the journey was easy, for we went the entire length of Port Meadow, to Wolvercote via Wytham to Botley, where it joined the Eynsham Meadow and then let Molly rest and graze at the Wolvercote end, so that Shandy could suckle and then have a little rest before the long stretch of the Wytham Road, which lay ahead. But Shandy didn't want to rest and after her drink she began to frisk about and play, so we caught her quickly and put her collar and lead on again – we didn't want her to be worn out even before we began.

The Wytham Road was a delightful, peaceful little lane that wound its unhurried way through water meadows from Wolvercote via Wytham to Botley, where it joined the Eynsham Road. The roadway was paved but most of the way there was a grass verge so Shandy didn't have to walk too far along the hard surface. Molly, of course, behaved beautifully, walking along at her quiet, swinging pace, and Shandy was quite happy to trot along behind her mother. We stopped often so that she could have a drink and Molly could nibble at the grass along the roadside. The whole journey was eight miles or so, and when we had covered about five miles we found a really wide verge that stretched down to a little stream and here we decided to give Molly her feed and have our own picnic lunch. Molly sank her nose gratefully into the sparkling, clear water of the stream and drank deeply. Her soft muzzle sent ever widening ripples outwards across the surface and we saw the tiny minnows darting back and forth, suddenly startled by this intruder in their midst. After her drink Molly tucked into her feed and we stood round her eating our sandwiches and drinking hot soup from the flask Mother produced from the tandem saddlebags. The sun was shining and the sky was blue. It seemed impossible to believe that it was January, except for the crisp edge in the air and the bare black trees that fringed the meadows.

Shandy had had a long drink at lunch time and nosed round in the grass. She was disappointed that we didn't let her loose but, although there was very little traffic on that quiet road, it wouldn't have been safe to let her off the lead. She did lie down for a few minutes, but wouldn't rest for long, so as soon as we were all ready, we set off once again on our journey. We kept

79

worrying about how tired the foal must be, and certainly, by the time we reached the main road, she did seem to be walking more slowly, her woolly neck less high and her curly little tail just hanging straight down, no longer held proudly behind her. At last we reached the farm. The gateway was set well back off the road and we led Molly inside and, after fastening the gate carefully, we led Molly up the field a little way before taking her headcollar off. Immediately, her head went down to the grass and she began to graze. Shandy was tougher than we imagined. We took off her collar and lead, expecting that after such a long journey she would flop down to sleep straight away. But not a bit of it, she stuck her head up and pricked her ears, then she shook herself and set off as fast as her little legs would carry her, galloping round Molly in a huge circle, with her short curly tail stuck straight out behind her! Round and round she went, faster and faster. Molly raised her head and stood watching her daughter proudly. Shandy's circles gradually diminished in size and suddenly she came to a very abrupt halt at Molly's side, stuck her head under her mother's flank, and started sucking vigorously! Only when she had drunk her fill and brought her dripping white muzzle out from under Molly's flank did she remember that she was just a little bit tired. She nosed around the grass near her mother and suddenly flopped down for a well earned sleep, the last rays of the evening sunshine catching in her fluffy foal-coat and turning it to gold before our adoring eyes.

Shaddow 10

Every day for the remainder of the school holidays Pip and I cycled to the field to feed Molly, put out her hay, and make sure she was all right. The old man who owned the fields would have been happy to do this for us, and, indeed, was a great help during term time, but we couldn't possibly have stayed away from Molly for a whole day even if we hadn't had to feed her, and we were also busy with the training of the foal. If young animals are handled regularly and trained to lead, as Shandy was, almost from birth, they take it all for granted and there is never any question of 'breaking them in' later on. It becomes simply a matter of carrying their training a little further and teaching them to carry a rider, for they already trust people and obey them readily enough.

Each day we led Shandy about for a while, picked up her feet and held them – as she grew older we cleaned them out gently with a hoof pick to help them grow in a good healthy shape and also to accustom her to having her feet handled in preparation for the time when the blacksmith would have to trim them up, and, later still, put shoes on her. We also brushed her coat lightly with a dandy brush. Shandy loved being played with and would come into the big barn where we spent hours playing with her and with the new family of kittens we had found there. I think Molly was quite glad that we took her precocious daughter out of her way for an hour or so each day and gave her a bit of rest! When school started again things were more difficult, but some member of the family went over to the farm each day to check the animals and feed them and talk to them so that they didn't feel neglected or forgotten.

Early in March, when Molly and Shandy had been over at Dean Court Farm about two months, we were approached by Mr. Howes, who owned a farm nearby, and asked if we would sell Molly. A thoroughbred mare of his had just foaled and had died giving birth to the foal, so he wanted Molly as a foster mother for his foal because at that time he was rearing it by hand and was having to feed it every two hours, night and day!

Naturally, we told Mr. Howes that we could not possibly sell Molly. That was just as unthinkable as selling any other member of the family would have been. However, we promised to lend her to him for as long as he needed her to help him rear his poor little orphan foal. First of all, though, we had to persuade Molly to take the foal and suckle it, and since her own foal was already two months old we knew this would be difficult. We took Molly and Shandy down the road to Mr. Howes' farm and introduced her to 'My Orphan', as his foal was called. Molly was very cross and wouldn't let the new foal near her. She became jealous and protective towards Shandy, and, in fact, thoroughly un-Molly like. We left her at the farm for two or three days and Mr. Howes tried various tricks to get her to take to My Orphan, but it was no good, she simply wouldn't have anything to do with it. We just had to give up, finally, and bring her back to her own field. Fortunately, just a few days afterwards, Mr. Howes heard of a mare whose foal had died at birth that day and was able to get hold of her to suckle My Orphan. This arrangement worked very well and his foal grew up big and strong and thoroughly well-nourished.

We had all thought a lot about Molly and how clever she was to produce a foal at her age. We didn't know exactly how old she was – she had been sold to us as 12 but our vet said 20 would be a lot nearer the mark! We decided that, whatever her age, if she could produce a healthy foal like Shandy by an unknown pony stallion running on the Meadow, then she should be properly mated to a really good stallion and so produce a really good class foal. Mr. Howes had a very good grey Thoroughbred stallion at stud at his farm called Clear Dawn and we thought he would make an excellent mate for Molly. When we approached Mr. Howes about it he said that although he didn't normally take pony mares, since we had tried so hard to help him out with My Orphan he would not only take Molly, but would reduce the stud fee for us. We wanted Molly's next foal to be born at a more normal time of the year, so that it would not be exposed to all the harsh weather that Shandy had had to go through, so we waited till early May before taking Molly to the stallion, hoping for an April foal the following year.

Now that Molly had a foal, of course, we could no longer ride her, since while the foal is very young it is bad for a mare to work as this affects her milk. Even when the foal was two or three months old we could not possibly have left her alone in the field when we took Molly out as she simply wouldn't have stayed there. It would have been too dangerous to take her along the road, following behind Molly, so riding was out of the question. We were very happy just looking after Molly and Shandy and teaching Shandy to wear a halter and lead about the field, but we did miss our riding.

Mother realized how we felt and she knew we would not ask for another pony as we hadn't any money of our own now to put towards the cost, so she started reading the *Livestock for Sale* column in the local weekly paper. There were quite often ponies advertised for sale in that column and sometimes they were not too expensive. One Friday in March she saw an advertisement that looked promising; someone on the outskirts of the town was offering two ponies for sale. There was a telephone number, so Mother telephoned to get more information about the ponies. Apparently one was a nine-year-old bay Welsh type gelding about 13 hands and the other was a dark brown 3-year-old New Forest filly, a little bigger. Mother arranged for us to go over and try the ponies on Sunday morning when Father would be free to come with us.

Pip and I knew nothing about the possibility of having another pony, so when Mother made her announcement at supper on Friday evening we were wildly excited about the idea. Father was slightly disapproving as he said we couldn't afford any more ponies, but he soon gave in and agreed that we could, at least, go and try them on Sunday morning.

For once, the week-end passed terribly slowly and Sunday took an age to come! But at last it did arrive and we set off on bicycles to find the address Mother had been given. It was a council housing estate and the man who was selling the two ponies lived in one of these semi-detached council houses. We looked around for a field, wondering where the ponies lived, but the surroundings looked most unpromising. The house was in a cul-de-sac and we noticed that there was an empty plot of land next door to the last house – just about room to build one more house, but that was all. Father rang the doorbell and a man came out to where we were waiting.

'The ponies are in this field' the man said, indicating the vacant building lot. 'Just wait a moment and I'll fetch the bridles'. We parked the bikes and moved over to the rickety gate leading into the 'field'. There is never very much grass anywhere in March, but this little plot was completely bare. The ground was simply bare mud, fairly hard at present as the weather was dry, but obviously it had been very deep and sticky quite recently. We looked round and spotted the two ponies over in the far corner. When they saw us they came over towards us and nuzzled our pockets, looking for food.

The man returned with two bridles and an ancient looking saddle. 'Would you like to try the little bay first?' he asked, untying the awful gate and going inside. We were speechless,

Shaddow

but Mother said 'Surely you don't keep them here in this little plot? Whatever do they live on?' The man looked round, surprised. 'Oh, I feed them all right, and all the people living in this street help. We give them potato peelings, and cabbage leaves and so on. They do very well'. He had put the bridle on the bay and led him out into the road. Then he put on the old saddle and motioned Pip to mount the pony. I must say that the bay pony didn't look nearly so bad as the poor little dark brown one. Being older I suppose he was better able to withstand the starvation diet they had been subjected to over the past months, and being Welsh, he had a good layer of stored up fat that he could live on for some time. He was rather smaller than we had hoped, since we were both tall for our ages, but he was a gay little pony and we liked him. Pip trotted him the length of the cul-de-sac and then turned round and trotted back to us. His little ears were picked up and he held himself well, moved quite nicely, and was easy to manage, so far as we could tell with that sort of a trial. I rode him up and down after Pip, and then we put him back into the mudpatch. Meanwhile, the man had put an awful great big bridle onto the dark pony and led her into the street. She looked like a skeleton and her thick coat was stareing and dull. It had a dreadful motheaten look that added to the general picture of dejection she presented. Her neck was scrawny and she held her head low to the ground; her eyes looked glazed and uninterested as the man slapped the saddle onto her back.

Pip rode her first, but she was obviously completely untrained. She offered no resistance at all but was simply uneducated – which wasn't surprising as she was only 3-years-old. However, she did know what you wanted when you asked her to walk down the street and trot back, although it seemed cruel to make her trot. After I had ridden her we put her back with her friend and fed them both with carrots and pieces of bread we had brought with us whilst Mother had another go at the owner. She told him that she would be informing the

R.S.P.C.A. of the way the ponies were being kept, because they were starving and badly needed proper food and attention. Father asked him about price, and he said he already had an offer of £45 for the bay pony and he wanted £30 for the dark brown one. Father said this was quite ridiculous, and added that it would be touch and go if the pony lived, considering its poor condition. He advised the man to take the £45 he had been offered for the bay pony and get rid of it before the authorities took it from him and took him to court for starving the animals. As we turned to our bicycles Mother said she would give him £15 for the filly which might, at least, save him from being prosecuted; but he was quite cross by now and also, I suspect, frightened, and said he wouldn't take it. Mother gave him a card with our name and address on it in case he changed his mind, and we mounted our iron steads and rode off.

We cycled home in silence, thinking of the two poor little ponies being slowly starved to death through the sheer ignorance of the man who owned them. All the neighbours who had come out to watch us ride the ponies had seemed to be nice, ordinary people and genuinely fond of them. Many had brought out tit-bits and the owner himself was not a cruel man – he had seemed proud of his ponies – just ignorant of the fact that they were being starved and that they needed a plentiful supply of fresh, clean water all the time, instead of half a bucket of dirty water, and that they needed plenty of good quality hay, at least, if not oats and carrots as well.

Mother was as good as her word and on the Monday morning she got in touch with the local R.S.P.C.A. inspector. He visited the ponies and reported back on the Tuesday that by the time he had arrived the bay pony had already gone to its new home, but he had done all he could to help the young filly and at least she had some hay now.

Pip and I returned reluctantly to our schoolwork and spent as long as possible each day with Molly, and it was not until tea time on Wednesday that there were any further developments.

We had just started our tea when there was a knock at the front door. Mother answered it and we heard a man's voice. We recognized it at once – it was the man who owned the ponies! Apparently he had been scared by the Inspector's call, for he explained rather penitently that he had not realized that the ponies weren't getting enough to eat, but that he had now bought some hay for the filly – the gelding had been sold. Evidently he had no use for the filly and really wanted to get rid of her as quickly as possible (perhaps he was afraid she might die!). 'If you want her' we heard him say 'you can have her for £20.' Mother still had some of the housekeeping money for that month in her handbag and she had not enjoyed having tormenting thoughts about the dejected little pony, so she said rather quickly 'I'll give you £17.10.0 for her, cash, but that's my final word'. And the man accepted! He wrote a receipt, took the money, and, after Mother had said that we would come to collect the pony on Sunday, and that meanwhile he must see that she had fresh water and fresh hay twice a day, he left. When she came back into the dining room we both hugged her. We, too, had thought a lot during the past few days of the dull, listless eyes of the dark filly.

By the time supper was over that night poor Father had listened to all the details of what the man said several times over and endured our excited babble about what we would do with the pony and how we would feed her up and make her well again.

'You must both remember' he said, when he could make himself heard, 'that this pony has been starved over a long period. It would be just as foolish to stuff her suddenly full of food as it is to keep her short of if.'

'Where shall we keep her, Daddy.' Pip asked. 'With Molly?'

'No, I think at first it would be a good idea to keep her on the Meadow. The grass won't be too rich there yet, but it's good grazing. All the horses do well there, and it will give her a chance to get well and strong quickly. Also it will mean that she's close to the house, which would be more convenient if we need to have the vet to her anytime.'

'The first thing to do with her,' Mother interjected, 'is to get rid of those lice! She was covered in them. I'll get some louse powder tomorrow and when you fetch her on Sunday you can wear your oldest jeans both of you and we can burn them afterwards if necessary.'

'Golly!' I said. 'How will we get her home?'

'Oh, I think she can walk if we take it gently. It's only about three miles, perhaps less. She's probably stronger than she looks and she will have had a week with some food by then.' Father seemed quite confident, and, of course, he turned out to be absolutely right. When we arrived at the cul-de-sac on Sunday morning the man was waiting for us. We had brought Molly's snaffle bridle with us because we did not want Shaddow, as we had already named her, to have to wear ever again the horrible rusty old pelham she had worn the previous Sunday. She certainly did look a bit brighter and it was obvious that the man had been feeding her some hay during the week, but she still made a pathetic little figure as we set off down the road. We hadn't bothered about a saddle as we didn't want to get Molly's saddle 'lousey' and anyway, Shaddow was so poor that she would probably have got a sore back or girth galls from wearing a saddle even for that short journey. So we rode her bareback, or walked beside her in turns all the way home.

We arrived home in time for lunch and it was lovely to have a pony in the garden again! Shaddow had been given to Pip as her birthday present and Easter present combined and she was just bursting with pride in her new pony already. Before lunch we brushed Shaddow gently with a dandy brush, and went all over her with the louse powder, paying particular attention to her crest, back and croup. Then we tied her up in the garden and gave her a small feed consisting mostly of damp bran but with some oats and carrots in it to disguise the flavour of the worm dose which was also added. When she had eaten it all up, we gave her some good hay and left her in peace whilst we got out of our oldest jeans and, leaving them outside, went in to wash thoroughly before lunch.

After lunch we led Shaddow down to the meadow and watched her happily as she smelt the wind of the wide open space and the good sweet grass and the wide river. Then she sank her nose into the cool green stems and began to graze.

Introducing Sparkie 11

As the blustering winds and chilly rain of March gave way to the days of gentle sunshine and showers of early April, Shaddow started to show a marked improvement. Pip didn't ride her at all at first but visited her every day taking her a small feed to supplement her grass diet, as we felt she needed protein badly. With the lice cleared from her long coat and the parasites cleared from her insides, she began to put on flesh rapidly. She was a delightful character, quiet and gentle and kind, with an amazingly sweet disposition considering the awful treatment she had received in her short life. She quickly learned to know that she belonged to Pip and would give a little whinny whenever she saw her approaching across the meadow and trot out to meet her. This was a pleasant change from the games we had had of old with Molly!

We did not neglect Molly, of course, now that we had Shaddow as well, but visited Molly and Shandy in the mornings and Shaddow in the afternoons; or, if it was a school day, I would cycle over to Dean Court to feed Molly, and Pip would go off down to the meadow to find and feed Shaddow. Soon, though, it was the Easter holidays and we had nearly four weeks to spend entirely with our ponies.

As soon as Pip felt Shaddow was strong and healthy enough she started riding her. She used Molly's snaffle at first and only rode for ten minutes or quarter of an hour at a time. She was a very patient teacher and would spend nearly all the time walking, teaching Shaddow to answer the lightest touch on the rein and to walk properly, using her back muscles and her hocks. Shaddow, like so many of the New Forest ponies, was rather long in the back and heavy in front, so that her weight tended to be too much on her forehand. Pip knew that she had to strengthen the back and neck muscles and develop the quarters before she could expect the pony to carry her slightly over heavy head correctly. Gradually, as Shaddow became more and more fit and April moved into May, Pip increased the work at trot and the resulting improvement in Shaddow's shape and the way she moved and carried herself, more than justified all the hard work.

I often rode on the meadow, with Pip, because I still had the use of The Witch, but she was now terribly fat and in grave danger of developing laminitis. Her owners didn't do anything about it although we warned them about her condition and asked if they couldn't move her on to some less rich pasture. When I didn't ride The Witch with Pip and Shaddow, I would spend long hours over at the farm with Molly and Shandy. Shandy had been given to me and I knew that in due course I would be responsible for her training. I felt it was most important that she should be handled every day and I led her about and picked up her feet and generally made a fuss of her for half an hour or so when I had finished brushing Molly. Then I fed Molly and mixed some damp bran with a few oats in a tiny bowl for Shandy and fed this to her whilst Molly was eating.

Pip had started to use Molly's saddle on Shaddow, and as it fitted her well and we obviously weren't going to be using Molly much, it soon became known as Shaddow's saddle. However, she found that the pony didn't go very well in Molly's snaffle bridle. Shaddow was getting so much fitter and stronger and Pip found she pulled against the snaffle and seemed to get more on her forehand as she leaned on the bit. We were rather at a loss to know what to do with her and when we talked to Frances about it one day she suggested trying Shaddow in a small pelham. Fra had used a pelham on a little pony she had had a couple of years before and found it most useful and now she didn't use the bit at all, so she gave it to Pip. It was a metal pelham, but with quite a mild, thick, mouthpiece and very short cheeks. Used with a fairly loose curb chain it gave just that little bit of leverage Pip needed and Shaddow seemed to prefer the straight bit in her small, baby mouth, to the jointed snaffle, which has quite a pinching action on the tongue. I'm not a great advocate of the Pelham bit, but the fact remains that for no apparent reason many ponies do go better in a pelham than in any other bit.

The lovely May days began to lengthen into June. It was going to be a glorious summer. Shaddow and Molly had both changed into their summer coats and Shaddow was nicely rounded and muscled up. Pip had started teaching her the art of gymkhana games and as this training followed on a really sound basis of training in suppleness and obedience on the flat, the pony was both willing and able to respond with agility when asked to turn sharply and stop and start suddenly.

We had many friends amongst the people who lived in Wolvercote and rode on Port Meadow, and we had come to know and respect one delightful old gentleman, Mr. Humphrey, particularly. Mr. Humphrey owned a lovely chestnut cob. He was an old horse when we knew him and I don't think we ever knew his name, he was always referred to simply as 'Humphrey's cob', and he and his master presented a delightful picture that might have come straight out of an old print. The cob was a perfect gentleman. He was about 15 hands and beautifully rounded, with a hogged mane and docked tail, as was the fashion for cobs then. Mr. Humphrey rode him magnificently, in the old fashioned style, with legs well forward, body very straight and leaning slightly back, hands held high. But he never touched that horse's mouth with more pressure than the weight of the rein and the cob was the handiest animal I had ever ridden.

Mr. Humphrey often used to stop and talk to us while we schooled Shaddow and The Witch or the little fat black pony we had also been given permission to ride, and he gave us a lot of help, advice, and encouragement. He kept the cob on the meadow and it seemed a long way for such a very old man to have to walk before having his ride, so one day we plucked up courage and asked if we could ever be any help to him by catching up the cob and bringing it to his stables for him. He seemed very grateful for the offer and in return he sometimes let us ride the cob. Riding this beautifully trained horse was our idea of heaven. He had a truly rocking-horse canter and his compact and heavy looking body was as light as a feather when you were seated on his back.

Mr. Humphrey's home was a lovely old cottage on the edge of Wolvercote village, backing onto the meadow, and he had a small stableyard at the back of the house. Everything about the house, garden and stableyard was neat and tidy, just like the man who owned it. As we got to know him better, we spent many happy hours with him in his stables and in his house, looking at old photographs of horses and horse shows and listening to fascinating tales of people and horses he had known. He had bred and shown cobs for many years and had some wonderful pictures. One day he told us that, as we were so keen on gymkhanas, he was going to lend us his little pony, Sparkie. Sparkie was quite old, too, and had belonged to Mr. Humphrey's daughters, but now they were grown up and married and Sparkie lived an idle life on Port Meadow.

'She isn't that old', he told us, 'a little bit of work is just what she needs. She's only 12.2 h.h. and that's small for either of you girls'. He eyed our lanky frames, 'But you need a small, nippy pony for gymkhanas and I know you'll ride her sensibly and have lots of fun with her.'

We felt tremendously honoured that Mr. Humphrey should want to lend his pony to us, and, as Pip was busy schooling Shaddow, I started riding Sparkie regularly with her. Fortunately Mr. Humphrey still had all Sparkie's tack because we wouldn't have had anything small enough for her. She was tiny, with a small head and a long, thin body, with a rather streamlined look about her. She was incredibly quick on her feet, and although I felt rather long on her, I certainly wasn't too heavy and it was so easy to jump on and off her when she was cantering. Shaddow rapidly improved in her bending race practices now that she had Sparkie to practice with her. The two ponies sharpened each other up and by the time July came, with the prospect of the long summer holidays, we were beginning to get really excited about the summer shows.

During June we noticed that Shaddow seemed to have some skin irritation on her crest, withers and croup region. She started rubbing these areas whenever she could against a low branch of a tree or a hedge, or a post, until she rubbed big raw patches on herself and her lovely dark mane was ragged looking and awful. We didn't know what to do about it or what was wrong with her but we thought it must be some infection of her skin, so we covered the raw areas with Green Oils (I don't think we could have survived without Petifers Green Oils, every scratch and cut was dressed with it, whether it was on us or the ponies, and the strong, distinctive aroma became part of our personal aura). When the patches didn't improve after a few days' treatment with Green Oils we asked the vet to look at Shaddow and he told us she had Sweetitch. We had never heard of Sweetitch, but the vet explained that it is a fairly common condition in ponies in certain parts of the country. It appears in June and disappears, just as mysteriously as it comes, in September. It is apparently caused by an allergy to some substance, perhaps one of the spring grasses, and there isn't really any known cure. The vet gave us some horribly messy dressing that was oil with sulphur in it, which certainly seemed to give Shaddow some relief, but, of course, we got covered in the beastly stuff every day and Shaddow looked and smelled rather awful.

Before the end of the summer term, Horse Show and Gymkhana schedules started to arrive through the post, and we spent hours working out which shows we would be able to get to and what classes we would enter, and so on. We didn't have a horse box or a trailer, and it was madly expensive to hire one, so we only went to shows that were close enough for us to hack to. The gymkhana classes were mostly in the afternoon and evening, anyway, and during August it stayed light till about nine o'clock, so we were able to work out an itinerary quite easily that would give us at least one show a week and not involve any hacking home in the dark.

What a summer that was! We learned so much. We took Shaddow and Sparkie to all the local shows and met and made friends with the local horsey population. Sparkie, of course, was an old hand at the job, and she and I together became unbeatable in bending and potato races. She was so small and could stop and start and turn so quickly, that it was hard for bigger ponies to compete with her. Shaddow was completely new to all of it, but in a very short time she had grasped the hang of things and she and Pip had such a close understanding that they automatically worked together as a team, always seeming to have the same aim in view and never wasting a moment of valuable time in competitions by working as individuals. Very soon Shaddow and Pip were becoming acclaimed at the local shows, and several people tried hard all summer to buy the pony from her. But the answer was always the same – 'I'm sorry, she isn't for sale'.

Most Saturday evenings found the four of us, Pip and Shaddow and Sparkie and I hacking home from a show with one or two ribbons each tied to the bridles of our proud ponies. How they enjoyed their rosettes! They held their heads up and walked with light springy steps, enjoying the admiring glances of passers by as much as we did. And we would hum happily to ourselves and watch the last of the colour drain from the summer evening, as we brushed and fed our tired ponies, before turning them out once again onto the meadow, and cycling wearily home to our long-overdue evening meal.

Despite our widened interests and all our new friends, Molly was not forgotten. We visited her every day and brushed and fed her and led Shandy about. Molly's white rosette still held pride of place on my rosette board above the piano in the living room, even though there were others there now, reds and blues and yellows, all hard-won and each a vivid reminder of some exciting contest.

September came along all too soon and school started once more. We returned Sparkie to Mr. Humphrey, with many, many thanks for making such a wonderful summer possible; and with many regrets, on my part, because I knew I was now much too big for her and certainly I would not be able to use her again next summer, even if she had been offered to me. In fact, Sparkie was destined to join Mr. Humphrey's daughter's family where she spent the rest of her life teaching a new generation of children to love and enjoy ponies.

Shaddow left the meadow, too, and went over to the farm to join Molly, who was already preparing for the winter and growing a long, thick, warm coat.

Hunting at Last 12

We had decided some time previously not to attempt to wean Shandy artificially, principally because we didn't really have anywhere we could safely put her if we separated her forcibly from Molly. In any case, we felt certain that Molly would wean her foal herself, when the right time came, and in this we were absolutely right. As the autumn progressed and we began to increase the amount of food the ponies got each day, we noticed that Shandy hardly ever suckled from her mother any more, but became increasingly greedy for her corn feed and the hay we put out for them. After a time, we noticed that even if Shandy approached her mother with an eye on the 'milk bar' Molly would lay back her ears and make such terrifying faces at her that she hastily changed her mind. So, without any of the battles and worries associated with weaning foals, we had this problem solved for us by Molly herself by the time Shandy was about 11 months old, and we had a fine, well-grown and healthy foal and a fit and happy brood-mare.

Our breeding programme was evidently going to put paid, once again, to any prospects of hunting, even had we thought Shaddow and Molly suitable mounts for us to brave the hunting field for the first time. Our disappointment must have been evident because, early in December, Father came home one night beaming and announced that he had arranged for us to be taken hunting by a man he knew who lived at Horsepath, just outside Oxford, and kept two or three horses for hire. It was not really a riding stable, but it suited us ideally. We were to be escorted out on half a dozen Saturdays throughout the season, and initiated into the 'do's' and 'don'ts' of hunting, so that when the time eventually came to take our own horses out with hounds, we would at least know how to behave.

The first Saturday approached, and daily our apprehension grew. This was what we had always longed to do. This was what we had read about, dreamed about, ever since we started to ride. And yet, as the time arrived to try the sport for ourselves we were filled with forebodings and the certainty that we would do something absolutely awful, like running into the Master's horse, or being bucked off before we even began.

Mother was never really in favour of fox hunting. Despite her Irish upbringing, I suspect that her sympathies were always rather on the side of the fox. But she knew how much we wanted to try it and she knew that it would teach us independence, courtesy, courage and quick thinking. She made certain that we were spotlessly turned out in our best jodhpurs and jackets with shining boots and polished Pony Club badges, and sent us off with Father towards the stables. It was a perfect hunting morning, that first Saturday. A light breeze blew the thin clouds across the clean, washed-looking sky, and the hedges and trees stood out black against the sleeping fields. We found that Mr. Grey had two very genuine and sturdy looking bay horses waiting for us, both about 15.2 h.h. and perhaps ten or twelve years old; very experienced animals. We mounted about ten-thirty, as the meet was at eleven o'clock, and not too far away, and, waving goodbye to Father, who was going on to the meet by car, we set off down the road at a gentle trot.

Excitement had made me feel quite sick that morning, but now there was too much to do learning about the strange horse I was riding and watching the unfamiliar countryside. I forgot all my fears, and settled down to enjoy myself, regardless –

99

determined that I would try not to make too much of a fool of myself.

The meet was held on a village green in front of an attractive old pub, and when we arrived it was already alive with people and horses and parked trailers, around which people were busily unloading or tacking up their hunters. Mr. Grey kept us well away from the main crowd and guided us towards a wide grass verge the far side of the cross roads. Our horses were not hot as we had come to the meet walking and jogging alternately, but they were now quite excited at the sight of other horses and the thrill of hunting, which hung, almost tangible, in the raw air. We walked about on the grass, and gave our horses an opportunity to stale, and gazed at all the people and the horses. Mr. Grey seemed to know a lot of people and said 'Good morning' to nearly everyone who came within hailing distance.

Suddenly, we saw Father coming towards us. He had parked the car some distance from the pub so as not to get it in the way at the meet, and was walking up the road. He was rather scathing about the people who had brought their trailers right to the meet, instead of parking them a little way off and riding the last five minutes; but his remarks were cut short suddenly by the arrival of hounds. It was the most exciting moment of the day so far. The Master, Huntsman and two Whippers In, in hunting pink came up the road with hounds obediently trotting along in a pack, yet absolutely ready to go the moment they were allowed. They stopped on the green and sat down or wandered about, never moving far from their huntsman, sniffing round the grass and the horses, and obviously dying to get started on the real business of the day. Mr. Grey edged us up a little closer and introduced us to the Master and the Hunt staff, and we said 'Good morning' shyly to each and hastily got out of the way. The Secretary came over to us and we paid him our 'cap', which, as Pony Club members, in those far off days was half-a-crown!

100

Quite soon the Master decided to move off. All the field hurriedly moved their horses out of the way and we, also, turned our horses's heads towards hounds so that they could not possibly kick one as it went by. We watched the hunt staff and the pack move off along a track across a field towards a little wood about half a mile away. Mr. Grey made us stay there until nearly everyone else had gone and then follow quietly along behind. Lots of people seemed to be on very over-fresh horses which plunged about all over the place and were a thorough nuisance, but our little mounts, though gay and obviously full of anticipation of a good day's sport, were obedient and sensible and trotted quietly along at the back of the crowd without any fuss.

When we came up with the rest of the field outside the first covert hounds were already inside working through it systematically, looking for their fox. We could hear the huntsman's voice encouraging them and an occasional blast on the horn, which made our blood tingle with excitement. Mr. Grey pointed out the Field Master to us and told us that he was in charge of all the mounted followers, that he would show us where to go and that no one must ever pass him, just as they must not pass the Master, or any of the other Hunt staff. There didn't seem much danger that we would do so! The Field stood in a group, mostly looking a little bored and chatting, but Mr. Grey took us a short distance away from the crowd to a place where we could see three corners of the wood and so would have a good chance, if we kept our eyes and ears open, of seeing the fox and also of knowing when hounds got him away and the chase began.

Neither of us really understood much of what was going on in the wood and if we hadn't been so excited just to be there, we might have been bored too. We were eager to be off, to try our skill across a strange country, and to sample at first hand the thrills of the chase.

After we had been standing around for about fifteen

minutes, and there had been one or two false alarms when we thought hounds had found a fox, the huntsman decided the covert was blank and called his hounds out on the far side. They started drawing along the thick, over-grown hedgerow towards a field of kale. We trotted at the tail end of the Field, through the wood and across some plough to the kale. Everyone stood alert at one end of the kale patch, as if they knew there must be a fox in there, and sure enough there was. Suddenly hounds were leaping and plunging through the kale, first one speaking, then another joining him and another and another until more than half the pack were on the scent. They drove the fox out of the kale and were off in hot pursuit, encouraged by the huntsman, who then blew the 'gone away' and the hunt had started!

Without knowing where we were going or how we would ever stop, we were rushing along muddy paths, the brambles and overhanging branches swinging in our faces and catching at our clothes. All I could see was the hindquarters of Mr. Grey's horse and the dirt flying in my face from his heels. My little horse kept close up behind his stable mate and Pip was close on my heels. The wind rushed past my ears as we burst out of the thicket and on to smooth turf. Everyone was spread out across the field and, galloping away in front, two fields to the right, were hounds, strung out and in full cry – surely that is the most beautiful sight and sound in the world, I thought.

There was a terrible congestion of horses at the far side of the field, all trying to be first over the hunt fence, a 'tiger trap' made of rustic rails forming an inviting jump built into a gap in the hedge. People were refusing and getting in the way, and others pushing through and one or two trotting quietly up and popping over into the ploughed field beyond. Mr. Grey stopped well back from the crowd and he watched the direction hounds were going and where the Field Master was leading the Field, and apparently he knew exactly where we should go when the time came.

'Don't panic' he said calmly, 'hounds will check up on the top there – even if they don't lose him altogether in that thick underbrush on the common, and we'll have plenty of time to catch up with them.'

He was absolutely right. He waited until most of the people had sorted themselves out from the 'tiger trap', then cantered quietly towards it and popped over with no hesitation, Pip and I close on his heels. We trotted through the plough. 'No sense wearing the horses out now, we may need their energy later' said Mr. Grey, and led us up a deep, hard-bottomed furrow. We rounded a corner of the hedge, went through a gate that someone was kindly holding open for us, across a road and out on to the common, where, sure enough, hounds had checked, and we caught up with the Field once again.

We weren't still for long. Hounds were soon off once more, but at a much slower pace this time, working their way courageously through the thick underbrush on the common. We all followed, more or less where they went, but sometimes it seemed to me we were going almost in the opposite direction to the hounds. However, somehow we ended up near them once again. Once we had a tree trunk to jump, and then, when the hounds got away on to some pasture, we had a trappy little stile in the corner of a field to negotiate. Both our horses popped over easily, cantered on, and quite soon we were in another little copse with everyone standing around talking again. Mr. Grey told us our fox had gone to ground in the copse and he didn't know if they would dig him out or not. I hoped they would not – it seemed more fair to let him lie. We moved on through the copse and out into a field. Mr. Grey said we could slacken our girths for a moment to let the horses get their breath back, but we didn't dismount as hounds were once more drawing the covert and they might go away at any moment.

The day continued in much the same way. We didn't have 'the run of the season' and, in fact, spent quite a lot of time pottering round the same few fields and coverts, but we could not have enjoyed ourselves more. We had heard the thrilling note of the horn and the huntsman's cry. We had galloped through the woods and across the fields. We had seen and heard hounds, however briefly, in full cry, and we had stood still and alert, listening, in a muddy lane, breathing in the smell of hot horses, watching the steam rising from their sweaty flanks. When, at two o'clock, Mr. Grey said he thought we had done very well and that the horses had had enough for one day, we were quite content to turn and follow him, walking quietly with long reins and slackened girths, back to the stables and a warm bran mash for our gallant mounts.

To Molly – Another Daughter   13

As Easter approached, our thoughts began to turn slowly, almost reluctantly, away from the delights of hunting, towards the summer shows. Molly, Shaddow and Shandy had wintered extremely well at the farm and Molly had now been moved into her own private field, a few hundred yards further down the road, so that when she foaled this time there would be no danger to the baby from the other horses. She had an open-sided shed in this field where she could shelter from the wind and rain, but she hardly ever used it, except to eat her feed and hay there each day, preferring the shelter of the thick hedge and the Beech trees around the field.

A small part of Molly's new field, close to the road, had been fenced off and there was a caravan parked in this enclosure. A friendly young couple lived in the caravan and they took a great interest in Molly. We told them all about her and they promised to telephone us if anything happened, and also to keep an eye on her at night. Molly should have foaled late in March, but March came and went and she showed none of the signs of foaling at all. By early April we were getting worried about her being overdue, and eventually asked the vet to come and look at her. He said she was extremely fit and healthy and that the foal would not be born for another four to six weeks. We were amazed that Molly could carry the foal more than twelve months, when the normal period of gestation for a horse is only eleven months, but the vet said we should not be concerned and that mares were great individualists, some foaled after ten months and some could go as long as thirteen months and still have a perfectly normal, healthy foal. There was nothing for us to do but contain our excitement and await Molly's pleasure.

During the winter I had grown 'like a weed' as Father put it, and it was obvious that I was now much too big for Molly, even if she hadn't been busy raising a family; and much too big for Shaddow, who belonged to Philippa anyway. I would be too big for Shandy, too, when the time came to train her, as she wasn't going to grow much above 12.2 h.h. or 13.0 h.h., but we decided that in two or three years' time, when Shandy was old enough to be trained, I should train her and sell her. We hated the idea of parting with our first beloved foal, but it was the only sensible thing to do as we were all so tall and she was so small. In the meantime, I needed a bigger pony altogether.

Just before Easter we heard from some friends that a small riding school about twenty miles from us was closing down – the young owner was getting married and wanted to sell to good homes the five or six horses she had been using. Father made some enquiries, and then telephoned for an appointment to see whatever ponies were still unsold.

We went over to try Charm the Sunday before Easter. The riding school was a rather tumbled down looking place, with fences and gates in poor shape, but the three horses we saw looked as if they had wintered well and were well cared for. The girl who was selling them met us and said that in fact she only had one left now, Charm, as the other two were sold and just awaiting delivery. Much later we discovered that she had sent her horses round to all the local riding schools and dealers and one had been bought here and another there, but no one had wanted Charm. Just looking at her with a completely

Charm

dispassionate glance I suppose I can understand why. In the first place her head was much too big. It was a lovely head, in its own way, but should have been attached to a 15.2 or 16.0 h.h. horse, and Charm was only 14.2 h.h. Her neck was just a bit too thick, and her back a bit too long, but she was deep through the heart, broad enough in the chest to be strong without being coarse, had good legs, surprisingly enough with no blemish on them although she was nine years old, or perhaps more. Her joints were large and flat, her cannon bones short and strong, and her feet were good. Her shoulder sloped well and her withers were well-defined and reached far back, promising a comfortable ride. But above all she was a lovely colour. She was a coppery chestnut with a very dark chestnut mane and tail, and a narrow, slightly crooked, white stripe down her face.

I gazed at her in admiration. I had not been expecting a beauty queen so I was not disappointed by her conformation. I saw only her beautiful, big, kind, tawny eyes set wide apart, and her expressive ears which twitched back and forth, lazily dislodging some early fly. She was already saddled and bridled, so I mounted and rode her about the field. She felt wonderful. In the first place she was big enough for me, and when I asked her to circle or turn right or left or stop, she did it right away, responding to my lightest aid, or so it seemed, after Molly and the little rough meadow ponies I had been riding in the past. She was much more comfortable at trot than the horse I had hunted that winter and when I sat down in the saddle and squeezed with my legs asking her to canter, she struck off immediately with the lead I had asked for. I couldn't believe it – it felt like floating. I pulled up and asked her to canter again, this time on the other lead. She did it, instantly or so it seemed, and we were floating again with that heavenly mane lifting and blowing in the breeze of our passing. I slowed down and trotted back to the others, glowing.

'I think she's wonderful' I said, breathlessly, beaming all over my face and quite forgetting all the discussion in the car on the way over about not saying what you really felt about a horse you were buying in front of its owner.

'Let Pip have a try' Mother said.

Rather reluctantly, I dismounted and Pip got on Charm. It was lovely to watch her riding the pony, almost as lovely as riding her myself. They looked absolutely super and when she, too, came back glowing, our parents realized they had to look no further for another pony. We left them to discuss all the sordid, practical details and we fussed round Charm, rubbing her forehead and stroking her shining neck.

Father arranged that Charm should come to us for a week's trial, during which time he would have our vet examine her for soundness. If she passed this examination, and if, at the end of a week he considered her suitable, sufficiently quiet in the stable, field and traffic, and not too much for us to manage out riding by ourselves, we would buy her. The price was the princely sum of £45.

Charm was to arrive the Thursday before Easter and Pip and I were at the farm early waiting for the horsebox. We knew it couldn't arrive before late morning, but neither could we contain ourselves at home, so we spent the day at the farm. Pip schooled Shaddow and I did some leading and grooming with Shandy, and then we both spent ages with Molly. At last we heard the horsebox and dashed to open the gate at the end of the drive. As soon as the driver had put the ramp down I went into the box to Charm's head, untied her, and led her out into her new home. Her head was up and her ears pricked. She saw Shaddow and Shandy and neighed loudly to them. She was evidently excited after her journey, albeit a short one, and so I led her all round the farm, into the old stables, and round the orchard. I showed her the stream and introduced her to the other ponies and all the kittens, and when we had all talked to her and stroked her and welcomed her (Mother and Father had by now arrived to welcome the newest member of the family) I took the lead rope off the headcollar and turned her loose. She trotted about happily, sniffed round the grass, had a roll, and then settled down to graze.

Pip and I returned later in the afternoon to check the ponies for the night and to gloat once more over the new arrival. Pip made lots of fuss of Shaddow and Shandy so that they wouldn't feel left out, but I couldn't take my eyes off my beautiful chestnut pony, and I could hardly wait until the next day to ride her.

Charm turned out to be everything we had hoped, and once again Pip and I were able to go for long rides together, exploring further afield now, round Cumnor and Boar's Hill and Eynsham and Witney.

I soon found that with Charm I had also acquired a new interest – Show Jumping. In 1951 Show Jumping was still a very young sport. Before the war it had been dominated by army officers and during the war the sport had little opportunity to develop. However, as the wartime restrictions gradually eased and a new mood of freedom and gaiety swept the country, ordinary people began entering Show Jumping competitions in small shows, and show organizers were beginning to realize just what a big attraction Jumping competitions could be. By no means every family had a television set, but even so Pat Smythe was already making quite a name for herself, and all teen-age girls who rode nursed secret aspirations to follow in her footsteps.

I had done very little jumping up until then, and I had everything to learn. Fortunately Charm knew a little more about it than I did, and together we managed to progress slowly. Most of our jumps were made of fallen trees in the orchard or of driftwood along the river bank on Port Meadow – hardly the most satisfactory training obstacles, but all we could muster. Actually negotiating the obstacles was the least of my problems; the difficulties arose on the flat. It took me some years to appreciate fully that control of the horse on the flat is the key to Show Jumping, but even in those days I realized that it was vital to get round the corners properly in order to be reasonably straight for the next fence. Unfortunately, what usually happened was that I could not turn Charm in time and we cantered straight past the fence. She very seldom stopped at a fence, but unless I was completely in charge, she ran out. I overcame this difficulty in a rather unorthodox manner – we trotted! I found I could turn the corners at trot much easier than at canter, and Charm seemed quite happy to trot up to the fences and jump them, so if there wasn't room to get back into canter again after a corner, we simply remained in trot. We eventually put up quite a good little course in the orchard, and I practiced two or three times a week. I was determined to enter the Junior Jumping (there were no Foxhunter or Junior Foxhunter classes then) at Woodstock Horse Show on Whit Monday.

The Easter holidays were over all too soon and we had to go back to school. But the summer term is always the best and it was lovely to be able to ride in the long light summer evenings. We had almost given up hope of Molly ever producing her second foal and we were getting used to her enormous and increasing size, when we suddenly realized one day that her flanks showed two hollows and the foal had dropped lower, into the position it adopts two or three days before birth. Molly was 'bagging-up' well (starting to produce some milk) and we knew that the foal would be born any day now.

Very early on the morning of May twelfth the couple from the caravan in Molly's field telephoned us and told us Molly had just produced a lovely filly foal. Apparently, they had checked her first thing when they got up and were just in time to see the foal born. They made sure all was well with both mare and foal and then telephoned us. Father telephoned the vet, who agreed to meet him at the field later in the morning, and then we had to go to school, so Mother and Father set off for the field on the tandem. They were greeted by a very proud

Molly almost purring with delight at herself, and a most aristocratic looking foal.

As soon as we got out of school Pip and I set off for the farm in great excitement. Molly was grazing on the far side of her field with her new foal lying beside her in the warm sunshine. We approached quietly, talking to Molly all the time, and she looked up towards us, her ears pricked, and blew gently through her nostrils, either to welcome us or to reassure her daughter that we were friends.

'Isn't she a beautiful colour' gasped Pip, gazing down at the bright bay foal. 'And look, she has a long white blaze just like Molly, but not so wide.'

The foal, who had raised her head as we approached, decided now that despite her Mother's assurance that all was well, it might be a good idea to be ready to run, just in case. She pushed her long forelegs out in front of her, gathered her ungainly hind limbs under her, and staggered to her feet in the rather absurd way very young foals do. Pip and I couldn't help laughing at her, she was such a darling.

'Hasn't she got unusually long legs?' I said. 'They're much longer than Shandy's when she was born. Do you remember what a funny, woolly little thing she was?'

'Yes, but this foal's father is a racehorse and Shandy's must have been a New Forest pony.' Pip was stroking Molly and gingerly trying to touch the foal as she spoke. But the foal was very shy and it took us quite a while to persuade her to let us touch her, and then she remained rather tense under our caressing hands. Her coat was soft and thick and warm, and her short, silky mane stood up straight from her neck, as black as her little curly tail. We had forgotten just how wonderful new foals are and we could not stop admiring her and stroking Molly and telling her how wonderful she was.

The vet had said that both mare and foal were absolutely fine and in excellent shape. We were feeding Molly two small feeds of concentrates every day so that she would have plenty of milk

112

for the foal. At last, as darkness fell, we gave her her night feed and set off home on our bicycles singing all the gayest songs we knew at the tops of our voices.

The other ponies, and even Charm, must have felt slightly neglected over the next few days because, inevitably, the new foal took up a lot of our time. We bought a foal-slip and taught her to wear this baby headcollar and to follow us as we led her along beside Molly. Quite soon she had complete confidence in us and would come trotting over to meet us when we called from the gateway. We could stroke her all over without alarming her and even pick up her feet in a few days.

As always, there was terrific discussion over a name, but this foal was to be Mother's and she had the final word.

'I think we should call her Joyous Dawn' said Mother. 'Her father is Clear Dawn and she was born so early in the morning.'

'But,' I objected, 'that's much too long a name for everyday use.'

'We can call her Joy, for short.' Mother said. 'That will suit her very well, for she certainly is a joy.' With which sentiment we all thoroughly agreed.

GALWAY COUNTY LIBRARY

Charm Makes Her Debut   14

After the initial excitement of Joy's arrival had worn off we suddenly realized that it was nearly Whitsun and there was a lot of preparation to be done for the Young Farmer's Club Show which would be held on Whit Saturday, and the Woodstock Horse Show, to be held on the Monday. In the end I decided not to enter Charm in the Saturday show because I wanted to jump her at Woodstock and it was a very long hack over there. Philippa decided to enter Shaddow in the gymkhana events at the Young Farmer's Club Show and not go to Woodstock, because she was getting very big for Shaddow and didn't want to hack her too far or ask too much of her by doing two shows in three days.

We all went to the Saturday show with Pip and cheered her on, and, as usual, she and Shaddow came home with several rosettes. One or two people tried to buy the pony, but Pip would not part with her and simply replied 'I'm sorry, she's not for sale,' as she patted the silky neck and remembered the scruffy skeleton of a pony she had rescued.

On Sunday I rode Charm as far as Port Meadow, as it would cut five or six miles off my journey the next day. It was, in a way rather a risk, because Charm could be very difficult to catch, but from the meadow it was only about six miles to the showground at Blenheim Palace and our class was not until the afternoon, so I felt sure that if I persevered I could catch her sometime during the morning.

I got up very early Monday morning and cycled down to the meadow to catch Charm whilst Pip went over to the farm with Father to feed Molly and see that she and Joy and Shaddow and Shandy were all right for the day. I took a bucket and a long rope, some oats, carrots and sugar lumps with me, prepared for a long seige. My fears turned out to be well founded, and it took me about two hours to catch Charm. She could be really infuriating when she wanted. She would come up to within ten yards of me and then turn suddenly and dash away if I took even the tiniest step in her direction. I could usually catch her at the farm because the fields were small and I could always drive her into the farmyard, but out on the open Meadow it was much more difficult. I eventually caught her that morning by putting the bucket of oats down on the ground, making a noose at one end of the rope with a running knot, and placing the noose round the rim at the top of the bucket. Then I retreated to the far end of the rope and lay down on the grass to wait. Soon Charm decided that the bucket was definitely tempting and edged towards it. She put her nose in and ate some of the oats and raised her head quickly. I didn't move. She put her head in again, for a little longer this time, and I got cautiously to my knees. She raised her head, but didn't run away. Next time she put her nose down into the bucket I tightened the rope gently and she felt it close around her nose. She raised her head, but not quickly enough for the rope to drop off and I wasted no time reaching her neck and putting the end of the rope firmly round it. When she had finished the oats, I put her bridle on and led her home beside my bicycle to groom her and prepare for the show.

I spent ages grooming Charm till she shone like polished bronze. Then I left her tied up in the garden with a small net of hay, while I went in to have my breakfast, wash, and change into my riding things. My class was not until half past three, but I set off about noon so that I would not have to rush at all and would have plenty of time for Charm to rest before going into the ring. It was a pleasant ride to Blenheim. I went across the meadow and then on to the main road from Wolvercote to Woodstock. There was a very wide grass verge all the way and shady trees bordered long stretches of the road. It was hot and sunny now, and we were both grateful for the patches of shade.

When I was about half way to the show, Mother and Father on the tandem and Pip on her bicycle, passed me and waved, and I was glad to know they would be there to meet me when I arrived. I was beginning to get the most awful feeling in the pit of my stomach – I was sure I would be sick before I arrived. This was the worst attack of the 'needle' I had ever had. Of course, I had never jumped in public before. My ex-Land Army breeches were thick corduroy and the long woollen stockings I had to wear with them were terribly hot. My 'riding jacket' was an old jacket of my brother's which had been adapted for me and altogether my clothes did little to boost my morale. However, my spirits rose as we neared the showground and Charm's gay mane danced in front of me. It would all be super fun – I was actually going to jump at Woodstock Show!

Father had found a shady spot on the rails where I could tie Charm, so I loosened her girth and took off her bridle and tied her up by her headcollar rope, and then went off to see the Secretary and get my number. I had a long time to wait for my class and I watched some of the show, but the sick feeling had returned and I was certain I was going to make a complete fool of myself.

Blenheim Park is the perfect setting for a Horse Show. The main ring, neatly fenced round with white posts and white rope, is smooth as green velvet, and shaded by huge old oaks and beech trees. Competitors are free to ride nearly anywhere in the park as they warm up, and as you wander through the lush green grass by the lakeside, feeling the warmth of the May sunshine on your shoulders and listening to the distant sounds of the military band and the announcer's voice over the loudspeakers, you know that summer has really come.

At last it was time for me to get on Charm and warm up. We worked for a little while on the flat, but I regret to say that I had only a hazy idea of what I should have been doing. Then we went to find the practice jump and jumped it a few times, just to get our eye in and tell Charm what was required of her. A moment later, competitors for my class were called to walk round the course, and Father held Charm for me while I joined the others and went into the ring to inspect the course. All the other competitors looked very old and experienced to me and the jumps looked enormous and incredibly solid. However, I walked carefully round paying close attention to each fence and which way to go after it. When I came out of the ring again I mounted Charm and went into the collecting ring to await my turn, which is always the worst part of the competition. I began to wish that the ground would open up and swallow me so that I would not have to go into the ring.

At last my turn came, and as I trotted into the arena the band started playing the overture from the Mikado. This cheered me up enormously and I felt that my career as a show jumper had really begun in earnest when I heard the announcer saying over the loudspeakers –

'The next competitor is Miss Mary Rose riding Charm.'

We cantered a large circle at one end of the ring and then I pointed Charm at the first fence. She went on willingly enough over the enticing looking brush fence and the red and white rails which followed it. Then we had to turn left and jump a stile in the centre of the ring, and, of course, we failed to make the turn and Charm ran out. A little breathless, I tried again, this time getting the approach straight and Charm popped over from a trot. We continued our round in this somewhat ungainly manner and I was finally eliminated after jumping nine fences because by then I had let Charm run out three times, and three refusals means elimination under B.S.J.A.

rules. I trotted happily out of the ring. By then I was completely breathless and exhausted.

'Golly' I gasped to my father who was waiting for me by the Out Gate, 'I had no idea show jumping was such hard work! It looks so easy when you watch other people doing it.'

I jumped off Charm, loosened her girth and led her to a space at the ringside to watch the remainder of the competition. There were several clear rounds and I gazed longingly at the youngsters in the collecting ring waiting their turn in the jump-off. If only Charm and I had been good enough, we might have been there too – might even have won a rosette. The thrill of show jumping, once experienced, would never leave me, and as I stood at the ringside I vowed that Charm and I would work so hard that no matter what disappointments, sweat and tears lay ahead of us we would overcome all obstacles and, at last, succeed as a show jumping partnership.

'Hadn't you better get ready for the gymkhana events? They're almost ready to start the potato race.' Pip broke into my day dream and I hastily mounted Charm and made my way to the gymkhana ring. Events here had only been waiting for the Junior Jumping to finish and now the mounted games and races were about to start.

Charm was nearly as good at Potato races as Sparkie used to be and now I was so tall I had no problem jumping on and off her, or leaning right over to put the potatoes in the bucket as we cantered round it. After three exciting rounds Charm and I swept home ahead of all opposition in the finals and jubilantly carried off first prize.

I had not entered too many events as I did not want to make Charm too tired. We won our heat in the bending race but were knocked out in the semi-final, and that left only the musical poles. Charm cantered round and round listening intently to the music. She was much quicker than I was in noticing when it stopped and swung in towards a pole straight away. Round and round we went, again and again, and each time Charm

118

cleverly reached a pole before our nearest opponent, until only two of us remained in the ring. Now we cantered in opposite directions to make it more fair, and when the music stopped, we both dashed for the solitary pole. But our opponent just beat us to it, so we had to be content with second place.

I gave Charm a breather after the exertions of the musical poles, and a short drink, before setting off quietly along the road home. Two bright ribbons danced on her bridle and my heart sang with happiness at having such a wonderful pony, and with determination to win the jumping class next year.

Another Meadow Drive 15

After Whitsun it didn't seem very long before the summer holidays were upon us. We were busy every evening with so many ponies to look after and we rode Charm and Shaddow nearly every day, as well as grooming Molly and leading Joy around the field, and also giving Shandy some attention.

When the holidays arrived we were delighted to find that Father had arranged some more jumping lessons for us at a very good riding school about twenty miles away. The Major worked us hard and was never satisfied until he could see that we were putting every ounce of our will power and concentration into our work with him. He was most insistant that jumping depends ninety per cent on work on the flat and we worked our horses for hours in trot, circling, shortening and lengthening the stride, halting and moving forward into the same rhythm trot, half-halting and turning, until they were supple and obedient and light. Then we would jump, perhaps using cavaletti or trotting poles and then working down the 'grid', a series of jumps built down the long side of the school at varying heights and intervals from one to three strides apart. The work soon began to show results on our riding and gradually Charm and I were becoming a partnership and could work together towards the same end instead of being two completely separate forces.

During the holidays we went to several Pony Club rallies and also to a number of small shows at the week ends. Charm and I often managed to complete the course in the jumping classes now, with only one or two stops; and towards the end of the season we began to get clear rounds sometimes. Then there was the terrifying and thrilling jump-off, and very often this would be where I made a mistake, probably through over-excitement and not concentrating hard enough. However, we did manage to win one or two thirds and fourths before the jumping season ended.

Philippa was growing very tall for Shaddow now and although she took her in one or two jumping competitions, she mostly stuck to gymkhana games. Shaddow's sweet-itch had, unfortunately, returned as soon as the weather got warm in June, but we dressed it carefully every day to reduce the irritation, and we all learned to live with it.

Now that we were based on the farm we didn't see the ponies on Port Meadow very often, so when we were told that there was to be a second Meadow Drive that year, early in September, and asked if we would like to help, we jumped at the chance. It was still dark when we set off from the farm on the morning of the Meadow drive, but even so we only just arrived at the Oxford end of the Meadow in time. It was fun to be part of such a large group of horsemen and Pip and I found ourselves greeted by friends we hadn't seen for some months. I thought what a long time ago it seemed since I had ridden Witch in our first Meadow drive, and what a lot had happened since then. Now I had Charm's well loved chestnut ears in front of me, pricking forward amidst her copper mane in eager anticipation. I hadn't seen the Witch for a long time and I wondered how she was and hoped that I might see her again during the morning.

The Sheriff and his officers arrived in their Land Rover and just as the first rays of sunlight penetrated the ground mist we all spread out along the 'bumps' and the drive had begun. We drove the cattle quietly up the Meadow to Wolvercote, letting the horses slip through our line, and then cantered back to start the drive of the horses, in small herds.

Pip and I went with a group of riders down to a lone willow tree that stood on the river bank about half way up the meadow. We had seen a herd of ponies there on our way up with the cattle, and I was fairly sure The Witch was amongst them. When we reached them I saw that indeed she was, but what a sorry sight met our eyes. The Witch had always had a tendency to be fat, like most Welsh Mountain ponies, and the grass on the meadow is lush and rich during the summer months, quite different from the sparse grazing provided by the mountains of her native land. Evidently her owners had not seen her for a very long time or they would surely have taken some action to prevent the suffering the poor pony was now enduring.

The Witch was standing in the characteristic pose of a pony with advanced laminitis. Her feet were appallingly long and she could not possibly have seen a blacksmith for months and months. Her head hung low between her front legs, her huge, fat, body was imposing an intolerable burden on her painful feet and she had stuck them well out in front of her. Pip and I were horrified to find her in such pain.

'Oh!' cried Pip, 'whatever has happened to her?' She jumped off Shaddow and walked quickly up to the grey pony.

'She has laminitis, I'd say,' volunteered a large young man on an old chestnut gelding 'and had it for some time, too. Looks pretty advanced.'

We had heard of laminitis and knew a bit about it in theory, but we had never seen a case before and stood in miserable silence gazing at the unhappy pony.

'What exactly happens when they have laminitis?' I ventured at last, and the young man, who was studying to be a vet, was happy to enlighten me.

'It's inflamation of the laminae, the sensitive, fleshy leaves

122

Poor Witch!

inside the foot. Normally these tiny leaves fit in between the horny leaves of the insensitive laminae, which are on the inside of the wall of the hoof. But when they become inflamed and swell, because the wall of the hoof is very tough and unyielding horn, the swelling cannot push outwards and the foot becomes so painful that the horse cannot put it to the ground. To try to avoid pressure on the inflamed parts the horse walks on the backs of its heels and sticks its front feet as far forward as possible. Eventually, the disease, which is caused by over-heating of the blood, and in this pony's case, gross overeating of rich spring grass, changes the shape of the foot. The toe curls upwards at the front and the wall of the hoof shows ridges all round it instead of being smooth. Finally, the bones inside the foot drop down, out of place, pushing the sole of the foot out of shape too. Once the coffin bone has dropped, there is nothing at all that can be done for the pony. It will never be sound again.'

The words sounded like a death knell in our ears, and anger and frustration rose inside us. How could people be so thoughtless. Ignorance was no excuse, if they owned ponies then they had a responsibility towards them, they could not simply abandon them to starve, or overeat themselves to death.

The whole party of riders had been shocked into angry silence by the sight of the suffering pony and the graphic description of exactly what had happened to it, but now someone shouted 'Look over here, there's another of 'em.'

We turned round in disbelief towards the shout, and saw poor old Joan, a very old pony we had learnt to ride on years before when we were having lessons from Miss Doerring. Joan was lying in the grass near the willow tree. She, too, obviously had laminitis. Her ragged hooves curled up at the toes, and her feet hurt her so much that, try as she might, she could not rise. For a while we kept on trying to get Joanie to her feet, but it was impossible. We tried to persuade The Witch to take a few steps, but it was no use. Both ponies were beyond help.

124

Sorrowfully, we drove the rest of the herd to Wolvercote and the leader of our party found the R.S.P.C.A. Inspector on duty. He went off in a Land Rover with his assistant and a humane killer and put both ponies out of their misery. Neither Pip nor I had the heart to go back with them, even if they would have taken us, though I was filled with remorse at abandoning The Witch at the end.

We hacked silently home, feeling sick and miserable. Our gloom seemed reflected in the heavy sky, for the clouds had come up and darkened the sun. They took on an ominous significance for me now. I thought of them as the ignorance and want of feeling and inhumanity of man, both for the well-being of the people and also the animals who share the earth with him. People simply couldn't seem to be bothered to carry out their responsibilities, and the result was untold suffering and pain. Joanie, we knew, was a very old pony indeed, perhaps nearly forty years old; but The Witch was just six years old.

Earning Their Keep 16

Our parents believed that the best way for children to learn the value and proper use of money was to earn and administer their own from an early age. It was by diligent saving of our small allowances and birthday and Christmas money that we had been able to buy Molly in the first place, and now Pip and I were finding out just how expensive it was to keep so many ponies. There always seemed to be bills to be paid – if it wasn't hay and feed then it was tack, or shoeing. For some time now our blacksmith had been visiting the farm regularly every six weeks, which was a little more expensive than if we had taken the ponies to his forge, but was essential because Molly's feet needed trimming and so did Shandy's, and it was too dangerous to take Molly along the road to the forge with Joy in tow. Early in the summer our finances had reached a state of crisis.

'We have to do something drastic,' wailed Pip, 'or we'll simply go bankrupt!'

'By my reckoning,' I countered, 'we are bankrupt already! We have to find a way of making the ponies earn their keep.'

'Do you suppose we might earn enough prize money at shows this summer to put things right?' asked Pip.

But with the average first prize for a gymkhana event at 30/– I couldn't share her optimism. In the past when we had needed money we had scanned the newspapers avidly in the hope of finding an advertisement offering a reward for the return of lost dog or cat, but we knew from bitter experience that this was a chancy way to make money since we not only had to find an advertisement offering a reward, but also to find the dog or cat before it returned home under its own steam. What we needed now was a good, steady income.

'I've had an idea!' Pip exclaimed, suddenly. 'Why don't we start giving riding lessons. I'm sure we'd get lots of the local children to come, there are always some of them watching us, green with envy; when we're riding.'

I didn't really like the idea of other children riding our ponies, not because I was particularly selfish, but because the very special and close relationship between pony and rider can be easily upset if the pony is handled by too many people. However, we could not expect our parents to continue paying out money to keep all our ponies unless we tried to help and teaching was certainly the best idea either of us had had.

Our first pupils were the Doctor's children who lived in the house next door to the farm. The girl, Wendy, was about the same age as Pip, and her brother, Tim, a couple of years younger. We started them off as we had been started ourselves, bareback, on the lunge. They rode Molly – she and Joy had been moved back to the main part of the farm – and sometimes Shaddow. The lessons were fun and, strangely enough, helped us with our own riding as we really had to think out the reasons for the system we taught in order to explain it to our pupils. We taught Wendy and Tim how to sit correctly, deep in the centre of the pony's back, just behind the withers, with their thighs close against the pony's sides, knees low, lower leg slightly behind a perpendicular line through the knee to the ground, and heels down. We taught them how to hold the reins, and then worked on developing their balance and grip by teaching them all the exercises we had learnt ourselves. As well as lungeing them, we led them about the field and the orchard and, as they became confident and more proficient, we let

127

them ride round the fields steering Molly for themselves. They made excellent progress and we were very pleased with our pupils, and delighted with ourselves, too, finding that we enjoyed teaching very much. I think Wendy and Tim received excellent value for money as at that time we charged only 3/6d an hour; but it is hardly surprising that Pip and I only managed to make enough money to pay the blacksmith's bill, even when the number of our pupils had increased to the point where we had to turn people away.

Inevitably, soon after the late meadow drive, the summer holidays came to an end and Pip and I had to return to school. I had privately determined to take Charm hunting during the coming season – everyone told me it would improve her jumping a great deal – but it was not going to be easy to find meets close enough to hack to, and, of course, I couldn't possibly afford to hire transport. The solution to my problem came out of the blue when one day I was talking to Mr. White, the farmer who owned the land opposite us.

'Why don't you go out with the Oxford University Drag?' Mr. White asked, after listening sympathetically to my dilemma. 'They often meet on my land, or just along the road at Tilbury Farm and you would have no distance to hack and you would also have the advantage of knowing the country backwards.'

'Oh, I couldn't possibly hunt with the "Drag"' I exclaimed. 'Don't they go at a cracking pace over huge fences? Charm and I wouldn't stand a chance.'

Mr. White laughed kindly, and then tried to allay my fears.

'The pace may be a little faster than an ordinary Foxhunt,' he said, 'but as for the fences, they are just the ones you and Pip jump yourselves when you ride across my farm. Perhaps you are not used to taking them so fast as you would do during a hunt, but I assure you it's much easier with hounds in full cry ahead of you and everyone else galloping along to keep you company.'

128

In spite of my fears, I was intrigued by the idea of hunting with the Drag and decided to find out all I could about it. Pat, the proprietress of the local riding school, proved to be a mine of information. She told me how the drag line was laid by dragging a sack along the ground and so laying a scent trail of aniseed for the hounds to find and follow; and how, in this way, the organizers of the hunt could arrange beforehand over which land the hunt would pass and prepare suitable fences, so that the patrons of the hunt would not be disappointed by getting too little galloping or jumping. Pat said that, of course, the whole thing was inclined to be rather faster than Foxhunting. The hounds had simply to follow a line already clearly laid and didn't have to worry about the fox going to ground or covering up his scent in a field of sheep, or anything, but she, too, thought it was a good idea for me to have a day or two with the Drag on Charm, if only for the experience.

The autumn drew on and the ponies grew thick woolly coats to protect them against the cold wet days of winter that would soon be with us. Even though I was planning to hunt Charm a few times, I thought it would be wisest to keep her living out as usual, as I didn't have much time for exercising during the week in term time. The ponies were fed every day, of course, and also had plenty of hay put out in the fields, but being out, they were able to keep themselves exercised and fit and didn't get over-excited and under-worked the way many children's ponies do when they are kept in in the winter and their young riders have too much school work to do to spend long exercising.

Pip was a little envious of my proposed outings with the Drag, but she had decided right from the start that it would be unfair to take Shaddow out with them, since she was too small to be asked to keep up with big horses going fast across country over big fences. On a Saturday early in November, when hounds were meeting at Tilbury Farm, I was invited to go along with them, and Pip came with me over to the farm in the morning to help me get Charm ready for the great occasion.

129

When we had finished grooming her till her, lovely chestnut coat shone in the wintry sunshine, and I had mounted and was ready to go, Pip got on her bicycle and came along the road with me to the meet.

Charm knew something unusual was afoot when we set about sprucing her up with such determination, and as we hacked along the road towards the meet she was gay and alert, pricking her ears more sharply as she caught sight of other horses and riders going our way. I didn't know if she had ever been hunting before, although I guessed that she probably had, and I wondered if she was expecting us to arrive at a Horse Show. Once at the meet, however, I was sure that she knew all about it. She behaved beautifully, as I walked her about a little distance from the crowd of smartly dressed followers on big, well turned out hunters. I was suddenly aware that Charm looked small and shaggy beside them, but her pricked ears and intelligent behaviour filled me with confidence, and pride.

It was an exciting day and the warnings I had been given about the pace being fast and the jumps high proved to be well founded. I kept fairly near the back of the field, out of the way of the subscribers and other adults, but Charm jumped so superbly that we never got stuck the wrong side of an obstacle, however formidable it looked, and so we were able to keep up with the hunt quite easily despite her small size.

I was so glad that I had followed Mr. White's advice and come out with the Drag which hunted over ground I knew well – it makes an enormous difference to the enjoyment of a hunt if you know the ground, as you know what lies ahead of you in any given direction and you can therefore decide whether you should slow down and save your horse if you get into some plough or heavy going, or if there is worse to come and you must press on or lose the hunt. In addition, if you have a fairly clear picture in your mind of the lay out of the woods and fields and the fence lines between the fields, you know approximately where the hunt jumps or gateways are and you do not waste

130

valuable time and effort galloping across a field in the wrong direction and then having to follow the fence line for ages to find the jump panel. Actually knowing the jumps themselves can help a lot, too, as you know whether you should slow right down, perhaps to a trot, because the fence ahead is trappy, or has a big drop followed by a turn; or whether you can safely canter on at a good pace as the jump ahead of you is a perfectly straightforward one on good going leading from one permanent pasture field into the next.

By two o'clock the hunt was over and as we hacked back towards the farm I was filled with a warm glow of satisfaction. We were both tired, Charm and I, but not exhausted; and we had acquitted ourselves well, thanks to her gallantry over fences, and thoroughly enjoyed our day. Pip was waiting for us at the farm and listened eagerly as I recounted every happening of our day while we both worked on Charm, rubbing her and brushing the dried sweat and mud from her long coat. Then we left her in peace to eat her warm mash, and when she had finished I turned her out with the other ponies for the night with many extra pats and thanks for having given me such a wonderful day's sport.

Goodbye Shaddow   17

Joy was at the chewing age! Spring was once more touching the hedges and trees with a soft, pale green, the sun had suddenly gained in strength, and she felt the surge of this annual renewal for the very first time. It wasn't that she was really naughty, she just loved to chew things up.

'I thought it was only puppies who went through this awful chewy stage' said Pip disconsolately one day after finding Joy busily chewing the flap of her saddle.

'Well, perhaps she's cutting some teeth' I replied, 'and needs to chew. We shall just have to be extra careful to keep the good tack out of her way. Perhaps all young animals chew things, but we just notice it more with dogs because they are usually around the house.'

Molly's tack was bound to suffer most of all because, since she was not in foal again, we had not weaned Joy and they wer' still running out together. We took the precaution of removing the leather reins from Molly's bridle and replacing them with baling string for a while until Joy got over the tiresome habit of rushing up to her mother and grabbing the reins in her destructive little mouth.

'It's really time we gave Joy a little more education, anyway' Pip remarked, and looking at the leggy, excitable, rather undisciplined youngster, we all had to agree. There never seemed to be time in the winter to do all the things that needed to be done with so many ponies, but now, with the evenings drawing out again, we started Joy's education a little more seriously. Of course, she had been handled from birth, but now we taught her to lead willingly and quietly, even going away from the other ponies. We brushed her each day, and picked out her feet, taught her to tie up in the stable yard, although we were careful to use a quick release knot and never to leave her tied up unless we were actually with her, in case she should panic one day and injure herself trying to get free. She was a determined character – I might almost say obstinate, but with quiet, patient work she became more obedient and sensible each day. She was, after all, only a yearling, so the lessons never lasted more than fifteen minutes, but a couple of years later, when we were teaching her to carry and obey a rider, we were glad that we had started her training when she was young, and had always handled her regularly.

Shandy Gaff was now two-and-a-half years old and was beginning to look quite mature. She was still very small and never, in fact, grew beyond 12.2 h.h. She had a fine, silky, dark coat, and long black mane and tail. We had continued her training whenever we could all through the winter, and although we certainly didn't intend to ride her until she was three and a half at least, we thought it might be a good idea to teach her to wear a saddle, and so get accustomed to the girth, before she grew too strong and independent. So one Saturday morning, after we had groomed her, I said to Pip 'You hold her for a moment and I'll fetch the oldest saddle we've got and we'll put it on and see what happens.'

'Let her have a good sniff at it, Mary, before you put it on' Pip cautioned, as I came out of our makeshift tack room carrying the saddle.

Shandy seemed interested in the saddle but made no move when I put it carefully on her back. She was so used to us leaning against her and putting the farm kittens on her back to let them play with her mane, that it wasn't until she felt the girth brought gently round her middle that she began to stiffen. Pip, holding her head, was stroking her and talking reassuringly to her all the time.

'Be careful not to stand directly in front of her' I said, 'in case she shoots forward when she feels the girth. I'll have to do it up just a little tighter or the saddle may slip round, but I don't want to squeeze her too much, or pinch her.'

'I'm O.K.' replied Pip, 'and I think Shandy's a very good girl, a lovely girl, and so grown up.' She was talking more to the pony in her gentle, crooning voice, than to me, as I gingerly inched the girth a hole tighter.

With the saddle in place, Shandy stood rigid. Her head was up and her ears half back. She just didn't seem able to make out what it was that was holding her firmly round the middle and she wasn't too sure she liked it. We knew that the explosion would come when she moved, and rather than frighten her more by trying to restrain her, or get hurt ourselves in the process, we simply undid the lead shank from her headcollar and left her standing in the farmyard with the saddle and the headcollar on. The gate into the orchard was open and the other ponies were there, so we knew that sooner or later Shandy would make a move in that direction.

After a little while, Shandy got bored with standing 'on the alert' and, finding that the thing on her back made no further move, she relaxed a little and dropped her head. Still the saddle did not move and she could see the tempting green grass of the orchard only a few steps away. Cautiously she started to walk towards the gate, but the strange, restricting feeling of the girth and the unaccustomed movements of the saddle on her back were more than any self-respecting two-year-old could tolerate without making some protest, so her head went down and her back came up and she plunged through the gateway and set off up the orchard, plunging and bucking, snorting and cow-kicking. Her little ears were pressed back against her head and

134

Her head went down and her back came up

her eyes rolled wildly so that the whites showed. Reaching the top of the orchard she stopped abruptly, flung up her head, wheeled round and raced back down towards the farmyard, mane and tail streaming in the wind. She bounced to a stiff legged halt, gave three huge cat-jumps, and stood quite still, blowing noisily through distended nostrils.

And that, honestly, is all the protest she ever made about carrying anything on her back. Finding that the saddle hadn't moved and that the girth was still in exactly the same place, she dropped her head and started to graze peacefully alongside the other ponies. We went up to her and caught her and made a great fuss of her; then led her back into the yard, unsaddled her and turned her loose once again. We saddled her every day for a few weeks and led her about with the saddle on, and she never again paid the slightest attention nor misbehaved in any way.

With the coming of spring our teaching business had once more begun to flourish. We found ourselves very busy on Saturday and Sunday mornings and Molly was very much in demand. Occasionally, we mounted some of the better riders on Charm or Shaddow, but Pip and I never really liked doing this because we did not look on our ponies simply as animals on which we could ride, but very much as partners and friends, and, no matter how careful the riders were, there is no doubt that having someone else ride your pony alters very slightly the communication between yourself and the pony afterwards.

Molly was in her element. All our pupils adored her, with the possible exception of one or two who came to us, thinking they were rather good, and would show us a thing or two, and who Molly promptly put in their place in her own delightful way. Molly was never impatient; she would stand like a statue whilst a nervous child plucked up enough courage to approach her and stroke her shoulder, and when that child mounted her she would move carefully forward with her long, easy stride, ready at any moment to stop and stand still if her rider slipped to one side or suddenly became frightened by the mere fact that they

136

were perched, somewhat insecurely, thirteen hands and two inches above the ground. But if her would-be rider approached with what she considered an over-confident attitude, mounted and then proceeded to ride her in a way which was obviously showing off, she would turn her head stubbornly in a direction opposite to that indicated by her rider and trot, or perhaps canter, very fast in the wrong direction, coming to an abrupt halt, usually obligingly keeping her head up, when she reached the hedge. If her show-off rider had been sufficiently humiliated by this demonstration of who was the real boss of the outfit, she would then behave like a perfect lady; but if the rider persisted in using undue force or in using the riding lesson as an opportunity to brag, Molly would turn and deliberately trot very fast down the hill towards the stream, where she would stop suddenly on the muddy brink, head down and ears flattened, depositing her rider ignominiously in the water.

The result of these tactics was that we had only very nice people to teach – the show-off kind came once and never again, or else changed character overnight and ceased to be show-offs. When it came to jumping lessons, Molly was the soul of discretion. We had built a small course of natural fences round the field and the orchard, nothing over three feet high and many of the jumps only twelve to eighteen inches. These little jumps were quite sufficient to give our pupils a tremendous sense of satisfaction and achievement when, after practicing each fence individually at trot and canter, they were permitted to pilot Molly round the whole course at a quiet canter. Molly still jumped well, despite her age, and it was lovely to watch the enormous pleasure and confidence our young pupils gained from riding her.

Pip and I usually took a sandwich lunch over to the farm with us on Saturdays, and after the teaching was over for the day we would eat our lunch, sitting on bales of sweet smelling hay in the barn, and talk about our plans for the summer. In the afternoon we rode together, sometimes schooling in the field

137

and then doing some jumping, and sometimes going out for a hack. Pip had grown a lot during the winter and was now much too tall for Shaddow, although the pony was capable of carrying someone considerably heavier, without any difficulty.

'I can't bear the thought of having to sell her.' Pip wailed, beating the hay bale with her fist. 'It's not fair. Why do we have to grow so tall? It will be like selling one of the family.'

'I know, it's awful' I said consolingly. 'But we have to face the fact that some day, some of the ponies will have to be sold if we are ever to be able to afford to buy and support bigger ponies as we grow up.'

'But supposing she gets a bad home, after all she's been through. I've just got her so that she trusts people again, and she's fit and well and happy. If someone bought her who didn't look after her properly I'd just die!'

We weren't the sort of children who thought that no one else in the world knew how to look after ponies or ride them properly, but we had, unfortunately, seen so many ponies who eked out utterly miserable, if not actually painful, existences, simply because their owners were ignorant of the most basic grounding in horse care, that we were frightened in case we should add yet another to their number.

'Oh Pip, I know how you feel' I said, 'But someone has to be sold and Shandy is still too young and not yet schooled, Joy is only a yearling and we probably wouldn't be able to sell her yet even if we wanted to, which I know we don't. After all, it is you who needs a pony and Shaddow is yours. Don't be too depressed about it. She's young, good looking, well trained and very successful at gymkhanas. We should have no trouble at all finding an excellent home for her at a good price.'

Pip was silent. I knew that one part of her heart thought I was a traitor to speak as I had, but the other part told her that what I said was common sense. On several occasions the previous summer a local dealer who had four daughters, two about our own age and two younger, had tried to buy

Shaddow. Pip had always smiled and said that she was not for sale, but when the new showing season got under way and we met all our old friends again and exchanged information about the new ponies they had bought, or our hopes and fears for the coming shows, she was constantly on the lookout for a suitable new owner for her pony.

The dealer, Mr. Vickers, was at the first small show we went to, and while we all chatted happily with his children he kept looking at Shaddow, and at Pip, and in due course he renewed his offer. Pip said 'No' more as a matter of habit than anything else, but this time he was persistent.

'Philippa, you must know you are really too big for her now' he said gently. 'I know I'm a dealer, but I also have a family, and that pony of yours is exactly the pony I want for my little Sue. Gill's outgrown her pony, too, but Sue is still too small for that one, and besides, she needs a pony like yours that already knows the gymkhana game but that is gentle and reliable.'

He was most persuasive and I knew that Pip was listening to him. It seemed to her a terrible thing to do, cold-bloodedly to consider selling one of the family; and yet Shaddow was not a human, she was a pony – a young, talented and successful pony. Whatever she thought of a man who made his living buying and selling ponies, she reasoned that he was certainly going to want the best mounts he could get for his own children. He would want them to win, for they were his shop window, and he would most certainly feed and care for the ponies they rode, since they were almost permanently before the public.

The following week Mr. Vickers arrived at the show convinced he had won his case. He brought with him a really lovely 15.2 h.h. thoroughbred mare, with four Derby winners in her pedigree, and suggested that Pip should take her in exchange for Shaddow. And so, finally, it was all arranged. Shaddow went home with the Vickers family and April Gift, the beautiful, aristocratic, temperamental thoroughbred, came home with us. Despite her decision to let him have Shaddow in exchange for April, Philippa didn't quite believe that Mr. Vickers intended to keep Shaddow for his daughter.

'He was just a bit too glib,' she said. 'I believe he had another buyer lined up for Shaddow, and a handsome profit into the bargain.'

I didn't want to believe her but the suspicion nagged at the back of my mind. Two days later some friends telephoned us to ask if we would sell Shaddow to them, since they had heard Pip was thinking of getting rid of her. We gave them Mr. Vickers' address and telephone number and suggested that they might call him to find out if he would sell Shaddow to them; then we would be able to keep track of her and would know she was happy in her new home. Our friends telephoned Mr. Vickers that night and discovered that he no longer had Shaddow – had never, in fact, taken her home, but had sold her again at the show, and had transported her to her new home that night. They persuaded him to give them the name of the new owners and then telephoned them, hoping that they, too, might be dealers. They were! Shaddow had been sold the previous day, but they could not discover who had bought her.

We never did hear of Shaddow again, but she was young and well trained and we simply had to hope that she would have been sold for a good price and would, for that reason if no other, be valued and well looked after by her new owner, whoever it might be.

A Real Show Jumper   18

It was now the spring of 1952 and it would be my last year in Juvenile classes. I, too, had grown very tall and was beginning to look much too long for Charm, but together we had made such wonderful progress that I looked forward to the show season eagerly. Charm was jumping really well now and we had complete confidence in each other. She seemed to love the glorious feeling of strength and power which surged through us both as she flew through the air, and our outings with hounds during the winter had given me a much better sense of timing, and greatly increased my confidence.

Charm and April soon became inseparable, which was both useful and annoying. It was useful in that if I couldn't catch Charm, which was unfortunately too often the case, Pip would catch April and lead her into the yard and Charm would immediately stop eating and rush to follow her. Once we had her in the yard, with both gates shut, she gave in and I could walk right up to her. As April was over 14.2 h.h. Pip wouldn't be able to jump her in Junior classes, but in any case, the mare wasn't the right temperament for a jumper. However, we set about getting the two animals really fighting fit and muscled up and we always rode to the shows together, Pip would take part in some of the gymkhana events, or in a handy hunter competition, and I would enter the jumping competitions.

From the beginning of that season we started to win consistently. Charm was magnificent. We would wait together in the Collecting Ring, each as nervous and as much on edge as the other, and then, at last, our turn would come and we would canter gaily into the ring. Really all I had to do was steer, and occasionally drive a little with my legs, and Charm did all the rest, with apparently no effort at all. She flew the jumps, springing powerfully from her hocks, and, hating to touch a fence, she tucked her feet well under her. Sometimes, if there was a difficult turn, we still slowed down to a trot, but the result was, almost without exception, a clear round. It was immensely exciting to know that we were now feared opposition; even local professional pot hunters with three or four ponies in a class became uncomfortably aware of us as Charm began to beat them out of first place more and more often.

'I simply have to win at Woodstock' I said to Pip one sunny afternoon as we rode together across the meadows which stretched between the farm and the woods on Boar's Hill. We did not go to shows every weekend for fear of making the ponies stale, or over-jumping Charm, and sometimes we went off for long rides in the hills, taking our lunch with us, and getting a much needed change of scenery.

'Why Woodstock in particular?' queried Pip 'Surely, whenever you go in the ring, you go all out to win. What's so special about that particular show?'

I felt in me a deep compulsion, but it was hard to explain. 'I suppose it has something to do with the fact that we really started at Woodstock Show, Charm and I. That was where I first felt the terrific thrill of show jumping; and also where we made such a mess of things due to my incompetence. And it seems a fitting sort of place to win, anyway, to prove to everyone that we intend to go on through the season, trying like mad, and succeeding!'

'Cor! Listen to her' Pip laughed in mock sarcasm. 'Don't get

142

so exalted you are ashamed to speak to me and April.' She 'whooped' suddenly and set off up the field at a gallop. 'Can't catch me, can't catch me!' she taunted – and of course we couldn't, though we followed in hot pursuit.

Despite the banter, Pip was with me all the way. She and April worked alongside me as Charm and I kept to a strict programme to ensure peak fitness in time for the Whitsun shows. I intended to jump her on the Saturday at a small local show which was being held near the farm, and then again on the Monday at Woodstock, so it was essential she should be really fit. By the week before Whit I was giving Charm three periods of fifteen minutes each at trot during one hour's work outside, going up and down hills as well as working on flat ground. I was also giving her two steady gallops a week, one a little over a mile and one a little under, with about half the distance of the second gallop at a rather faster pace. Charm was really well muscled up, and her lungs and heart were in top condition. I felt certain that she was in the best possible condition to start the jumping season.

The weather, as always, was perfect at Whit, and Pip and I had a thoroughly enjoyable day at the small local show we attended on the Saturday. Charm put up a splendid performance in the jumping competition and won it after jumping three clear rounds. We all had some fun in two or three gymkhana events, and Pip and April did wonderfully well in the musical poles considering April was new to this sort of thing, and carried off second prize. We did not stay late at the show, but took our horses home before they got tired.

I did not want to risk a repetition of the performance I had been through with Charm on the Meadow the previous year, and it would have been simply awful if I hadn't managed to catch her in time, so Father had arranged with a farmer friend near Blenheim Palace for us to borrow two loose boxes for two nights, and Pip and I hacked over there on a glorious, sunny, Whit Sunday morning. We bedded down the comfortable,

143

airy, boxes and gave April and Charm their lunch. Then we happily cleaned our tack and put it away ready for the show the next day. Later in the afternoon we groomed both animals thoroughly and washed their tails and told them both how important it was for them to keep clean during the night. Finally, around six o'clock, we fed them, and, leaving them contentedly munching their hay, we set off to the main road where we could catch the bus back home.

Next morning we arrived at the farm early, mucked out the boxes and fed and groomed the two horses. We had plenty of time to spare as the farm was less than a mile from the show ground, and my class was not scheduled to begin until nearly midday. When we felt certain that no more gleam could be added to either of our mounts, and they had had a good two hours to digest their breakfast, we tidied ourselves up as much as we could, saddled up, and rode quietly over to the horse show. Pip held Charm and April whilst I fetched our numbers from the Secretary's tent, and then she tied April to the fence and I remounted Charm and began to 'work her in'.

'Pip, will you come over to that open piece of ground and help me school, please?' I had discovered by now the inestimable value of someone on the ground whenever you are preparing a horse for an event.

'Yes, of course. I'm sure April will be all right where I've tied her and anyway, Father and Mother will be here any minute I should think.' She followed me across the springy turf to an open area some distance from the ring where there were not too many horseboxes or competitors and we started to work together on Charm's preparation for the ring. I trotted in large circles around Pip, lengthening and shortening Charm's stride, half-halting from time to time to close her up together, and then halting and moving forward into the same rhythm trot.

'She's still not really working with the inside hock' Pip warned. 'Why not try one or two rein back and then forward into trot exercises on each rein?'

144

A clear round in very good time

The rein back, when followed by the spring forward directly into trot, made certain that Charm was going well, was supple and obedient to my aids, and it helped her to flex and supple her hocks in preparation for the great efforts required of them in jumping. After working in trot, with a couple of periods of rest at the walk on a long rein, for about half an hour, I worked for a while in canter, still circling, increasing and decreasing speed and length of stride, halting from canter and moving off into canter once again, sometimes on the same lead, sometimes on the opposite one, turning my circle into a small figure of eight. After a little while I felt certain that Charm was attentive and would respond to the lightest pressure asking for increased forward movement or a turn or a halt, and I walked again, just as the announcer called my class into the collecting ring. I still hadn't jumped anything, so Pip and I went off in search of the practice fence, which Charm jumped very well five or six times, and then I rode her on into the collecting ring.

There was a big entry in my class, but I had managed to put my name down about sixth on the order of going, so I kept Charm moving inside the collecting ring, in case she should go to sleep before her turn. The atmosphere was rather tense, many of my fellow competitors were well known to me, but we didn't chat much – each of us was concentrating on the job ahead. We had all walked the course and I felt confident that Charm would jump well as the jumps were solidly built, with good spacing and no difficult ground lines, but I knew that several of the jumps were bigger than she was used to and that I would have to ride even more accurately than usual.

I watched the competitors who went before me and noticed the places on the course where they found difficulties. There was one rather difficult turn to the narrow style after two easy but big fences on the side of the ring, and one or two people refused the style because they came round the corner too fast and their ponies arrived at it unbalanced. The wall, too, was claiming

146

one or two victims, as it was high for a Junior class, and being solid and glaring red and white in the sunshine, it required a bold pony to take it in his stride.

At last it was our turn, and once Charm and I were in the ring I forgot everything else in the world. I was totally unaware of the crowd at the ringside, the band or the other horses. All that existed in the whole universe was that course, and Charm and myself. We set off confidently over the first fence and because the job in hand had our complete attention and we were by now a team and not two individual beings, we jumped a good clear round. Suddenly, I was aware of applause and I was riding out of the ring. I dismounted and slackened the girth – we would have to go round again in the jump-off, but that would not be for at least forty minutes as there was a very big entry. All the family made a great fuss of Charm as we stood at the ringside watching the other competitors. I felt jubilant at the way Charm had jumped, but also keyed-up at the thought of the coming jump-off – we hadn't won yet, not by a long way.

There were twelve clear rounds, so unless we jumped clear again we could easily be out of the running. While the fences were being raised I remounted Charm and warmed her up a bit and went with Pip to the practice fence, which Pip raised quite high for us so that Charm could get her eye in over higher fences before we went into the ring. We were second into the ring for the jump-off and I need not have been so anxious, Charm jumped another faultless round with as little apparent effort as the first, and we were now definitely through to the prize money as only five competitors had gone clear a second time. Once again the fences were raised and this second jump-off was over a shortened course and against the clock. Speed was not Charm's strongest point, but she was well balanced now and very clever on her feet thanks to all the schooling on the flat that we had done, so I knew I could cut corners without getting into trouble over the jumps. I had to go first in this second jump-off, which was a disadvantage because I did not know what time I had to beat, but knowing Charm I decided to jump the course at my normal speed, taking care to cut the turns as sharply as possible, rather than try to gallop round, which would probably result in knocking down a fence.

Once in the ring I was surprised to feel how keen Charm was. She seemed to know instinctively that this was the crucial test and that she must now give of her very best. She went superbly again, cutting the turns even closer than I had dared to hope, and although we didn't try to hurry, we kept up a good rhythmic pace and the result was a clear round in a very good time. To my huge delight and surprise I heard my name being called over the loudspeaker as the winner of the competition. For a moment I just stood there, unable to believe it. Then I flung my arms round Charm's neck and hugged her.

'We won, we won! Charm you are the best pony in the world. Our first big win at a big show!'

I rode her proudly into the ring to collect our very first B.S.J.A. rosette, and Charm showed off to the crowd like mad, tossing her head and bouncing along. She knew perfectly well that she had won and she intended to make the very most of her moment of triumph.

The rest of the day passed in a haze of happy sunshine. Both Pip and I went in some gymkhana events, and we both won two or three rosettes, including another first in the musical poles for Charm, who was a very versatile pony. At the end of the day we rode back to the farm, where the ponies were to spend a second night, immensely proud of our mounts, who stepped along gaily, ears pricked, and ribbons fluttering from their bridles.

That was the start of a golden summer for Charm and me. We had finally developed that elusive quality which you will find present in all successful horse and rider combinations in any competitive field, a real partnership, so that each knew the thoughts of the other and both worked unstintingly towards the same goal. With that sort of relationship, nothing could stop us, and very seldom were we beaten out of first place.

Only one cloud darkened our sunny sky and that was the fact that we had to leave the farm. We had known ever since the day we arrived there that the land was actually already sold for building development, but we had hoped it might not be used for a few more years yet. However, we were unlucky and we simply had to take a month's notice and leave. It was at this point that we realized just how overstocked we were. When your animals are scattered about the fields and orchard and farm yard, somehow there don't seem to be that many of them, but if you suddenly find you have to move them, and you have nowhere to go, you become acutely aware of each one. The problem of having horses and not having a place to keep them is a recurring one if you live in a large and ever growing city like Oxford; and we were no longer panicked by it. In the end we decided to move back to the Meadow and we rented three large loose boxes in a private yard in Wolvercote, as this would give us a base, and a tack room, and stables for bad weather and also grazing rights on Port Meadow.

The move was not difficult. We had grown up so much in the intervening years that we did not find the journey along the Wytham road leading Molly and Shandy and Joy an adventure any more. But it was exciting, in a way, to lead them out on to the Meadow and set them loose there, where all our riding activities had begun, oh, so many years ago. We returned to the farm and rode Charm and April sadly out of the gate for the very last time. Of course, we had to leave all the farm kittens behind and we had to say goodbye to many friends we had made in the neighbourhood; but we still had the summer holidays ahead of us, and looking forward to all the fun we were going to have with our ponies, it was impossible for our spirits to remain dampened for long.

Too Many Ponies   19

The yard where we were renting stabling was privately owned now, but it was the very same yard that we had known in the past as a Riding School and where we had first met Molly so long ago. Here we had slaved happily on Saturdays and Sundays, catching ponies and grooming and saddling them; helping water and feed the horses and clean the tack at the end of the day; and Pip remembered vividly that fantastic day when she had ridden out of the yard on Molly knowing that for the very first time she really owned a pony.

The riding school had moved now, and at first it seemed strange to be back in the old yard, which was the same, and yet somehow so different. We soon made friends with two girls who lived nearby and kept ponies on the Meadow, and the four of us became inseparable companions. The summer holidays had never been so much fun. Every pleasure is increased by sharing, and Susan and Jan and Pip and I were constantly up to something. Jan's pony, Bishop, was a sturdy 13.2 h.h. cob and he was a 'ride and drive' pony. He pulled a small governess cart and we spent many happy hours trotting round the lanes, his strong roan figure ahead of us between the shafts.

It was a long, hot summer, so our usual routine for the day was to cycle to the stables and then go out together to catch up the ponies; Molly, Charm and April, Misty, Susan's pony, and

Bishop. Then we rode, with Jan riding Molly, and afterwards we turned all the ponies out again except Bishop. If the flies were bad, we kept the ponies in their loose-boxes until late afternoon instead of turning them out as soon as we had finished riding. After our ride we would go to the village shop to buy our favourite lunch – a bottle of pop and some chocolate biscuits (we had sandwiches with us from home for the first course). Then we would sit in the shade of the overhanging stable roof, or on a stack of sweet-smelling bales of hay in the haybarn, and watch the sun bake the small gravel out in the centre of the yard, and listen to all the lazy, insect sounds of midsummer afternoons. We talked endlessly of our hopes and fears, of plans, of the future, and of the past. Later on, when the sun had lost its fierceness, we would harness Bishop to the trap and trot off on a jaunt round the countryside. And finally we turned all the ponies back on to the meadow and cycled home in the gathering dusk, still talking incessantly. We parted reluctantly, already looking forward to the next day and our ride along the banks of the slow moving, sparkling waters of the Thames.

Preparation for the weekend shows became more fun than ever now there were four of us. We could practice against each other and sharpen up our ponies without any danger of staleness. The big show of the summer was the Oxford City Horse Show, held on August Bank Holiday Monday, which not only had a Junior Jumping class with a huge silver trophy, the Lord Bicester Challenge Cup, reputed to be worth fifty guineas – but also had a full scale Fancy Dress class. I secretly determined to win the Lord Bicester Cup, but it seemed a bit conceited to voice this decision, so I concentrated with the others on evolving the most glamorous fancy dress costume possible with very little money.

'We've had the most wonderful idea!' exclaimed Pip, one hot afternoon. 'Susan and I are going to be part of a circus. I shall be a 'bareback rider' and I'll ride Misty standing up. And Susan

151

will be a clown and run along beside Misty, or lead him
perhaps. He will be ideal as a circus pony. He's lovely and round
to stand on and such a super dapple grey.'

'But how on earth are you going to ride standing up! After
all, you really aren't a circus girl and you don't know how to do
it.' I objected.

'We've got plenty of time' said Pip, determinedly. 'I'll
practice and practice until I can. It can't be all that difficult
really.'

'Pip's had a super idea for a costume' chimed in Sue. 'She's
going to make it all of coloured crepe paper. It should be easy
to do and think how cheap it will be.'

'Suppose it rains' said Jan. 'You'll melt!' and we all laughed
like anything because we thought it was impossible for it to
rain. The sun shone permanently from a burning blue sky day
after day. There had never been such a heatwave.

Susan and Pip worked hard every day after that, training
Misty to carry a rider standing up, and training Pip to keep her
balance while he walked along. Misty was only five and all this
was a new idea to him, but he quickly learnt the very valuable
lesson which every young pony should know: never be
surprised at anything your owner does.

August Bank Holiday Saturday was a glorious day, but it
was the last day of the fantastic heat wave, which broke on the
Sunday in torrents of rain. The Young Farmer's Club show
was held traditionally on the Saturday and although it meant
two shows in one weekend, the ponies were fit enough to stand
it and we turned out in force to support it. Once again, Charm
and I won the Junior Jumping and she went so well that I had
high hopes of winning the Lord Bicester trophy on the
Monday. We all had enormous fun and a certain amount of
success in the gymkhana events, and Pip and April surprised
everyone by winning the apple bobbing race in which you have
to bob an apple out of a bucket of water without using your
hands, remount, and carry the apple in your mouth back over

the starting line. We did not stay late at the show, but took our horses home before they got tired or bored.

After Sunday's rain, Monday was fitfully sunny with heavy, thundery showers. However, the morning showed a few patches of blue sky, so we set off for the City Show with some hopes that we wouldn't get completely soaked.

It doesn't seem to matter how much you win, in a sport like Show Jumping, for you never lose the thrill and excitement of competition. So many factors enter into it, not the least being luck, that I cannot imagine anyone becoming complacent or over-confident. Certainly I was feeling neither of these emotions as I prepared for my turn. But Charm was on a winning streak and she always hated to touch a jump, so she jumped a beautiful clear round, followed by another, and by yet another, winning the competition without difficulty and putting the coveted silver trophy into my grateful hands for one blissful year.

The lunch interval came directly after the Junior Jumping and the Fancy Dress class was to be the first in the main ring after lunch. We gulped down a few sandwiches and rushed about, getting ourselves and the ponies ready, and Mother had just helped Pip to dress in her bright paper costume when the rain started.

'It's not going to be much,' asserted Pip, 'just a shower.' and she vaulted nimbly onto Misty's rather slippery back and, in another moment was standing proudly erect and confident as Misty and Sue walked off into the main ring. But it wasn't just a shower, and we watched, horrified, as the downpour dissolved the beautiful paper costume. The crowd yelled its approval of Pip's accomplishment in riding standing up, and then started to roar with laughter at her embarrassment as her costume disintegrated. There was no doubt in my mind that Pip and Susan should have won that class, but the judges thought otherwise and did not even award them a rosette for their efforts. Evidently other people agreed with me as the crowd in

153

the stands applauded loudly as the trio left the ring, Pip still standing erect on Misty, with only bedraggled, soggy remnants of circus girl attire clinging to her white underwear.

The rest of the afternoon was rather an anti-climax, and as soon as we decently could, we packed up and headed the ponies back to the stables for a well earned feed and rub down. When we turned them out on to the Meadow, the evening sky had cleared and only a few pink and orange streamers of cloud lingered on the western horizon. Overhead the clear, translucent blue stretched back to the banked purple of the night sky coming up in the east. We four leaned contentedly on the gate that led from the paddock at the back of the stables out on to the Meadow and watched our tired but happy ponies sniff at the fresh, green grass and then, one by one, get down to roll in its cool dampness, before settling to the important business of the night – eating!

'I can't believe the summer's past already.' I groaned on the inevitable day in mid-September when Pip and I had to go back to school. 'It seems such a waste to spend all day inside.'

'I know' said Pip, 'but the evenings are still light enough for us to have time to ride if we hurry.'

It was true that if we dashed straight from school to the Meadow and were lucky enough to find the ponies quickly, there was time to have a half hour hack, bring them in to the stables for a small feed, turn them out again and dash back home before it got dark.

During October, Mother had to go to Ireland to stay with our Grandmother, who was ill, and while she was still away, early in November, the weather turned a little cold. Pip immediately started worrying about April.

'She'll catch pneumonia, I know she will!' wailed Pip. 'All the other ponies have grown thick, woolly coats to protect them from the cold and wet, but April is such a thin skinned thoroughbred – she scarcely has any coat at all.'

154

Thud against the ample quarters of the Colonel's horse

Pip fretted so much that finally Father agreed to let us bring April into one of the loose boxes. So the following Saturday, after we had ridden, we fed the ponies and turned them all out except April, and she remained, like a pampered princess, knee deep in golden wheat straw, with her aristocratic head looking out over the half-door of her box. It was about four o'clock when we had turned the other ponies out and they had all behaved perfectly normally, rolling and then going off to start grazing, except for Charm. She stood pressed against the paddock gate, ears pricked towards the stable, whinnying to April incessantly. April, of course, replied to every heart-rending neigh, and neither horse would settle down to eat nor allow anyone else to do so! We stuck the noise for an hour and a half, and they were still at it.

'Whatever can we do?' I asked, knowing that there was really only one solution. 'If we try to make Charm stay outside and shut April in, Charm will certainly starve to death and April will get no rest at all.'

'Oh, I don't suppose she would really starve' said Pip. 'Horses very seldom do, but it certainly isn't doing either of them any good as things are. We can't turn April out because it's too cold, so the obvious thing to do is to bring Charm in too.'

Charm was delighted. She settled down in her comfortable, sweet-smelling box next door to April, and a happy little smiled played round her lips as she nuzzled my pocket for tit bits when I went in to bid her goodnight.

The only snag to this arrangement was that our house was nearly two miles away from the stables, and the horses had to be mucked out, fed and exercised before school each morning, and then bedded down and fed again in the evening. However, although it is always quite impossible to drag yourself out of bed on a chilly winter morning in the dark to go to school, I found it quite easy to get up at six thirty for the sake of the ponies. I arrived at the stables before seven, did the chores, and

156

went out for forty-five minutes exercise riding Charm and leading April. Then I did the ponies over briskly and left them with a plentiful supply of hay, and cycled swiftly back home, changed and gulped some breakfast, and dashed to school by nine o'clock. I often took Paddy, our Irish Setter, to the stables with me in the mornings, as he loved the exercise and if I held on to his lead he would gallop terribly fast and tow me along on my bicycle any time I got tired of pedalling.

When Mother returned home from Ireland, late in November, the cold spell was over and the weather was once again damp and fairly mild. She was not at all amused to find that in her absence we had been stupid enough to bring two of the ponies inside, but it was too late then to turn them out again, and we decided we would just have to live through the winter as best we could and turn them out as early as possible in the spring. One splendid aspect of having Charm and April stabled was that we were able to ride out on to the Meadow to find Molly and Shandy and Joy each morning (often Pip and I went to the stables together in the mornings). And later on, when the weather got bad again, we fed them each day to supplement the grass and the hay which was put out for all the animals on the Meadow daily during the winter.

'As we have the ponies stabled and eating us out of house and home,' said Pip one day, 'why don't we do as we've always wanted and take our own horses hunting?'

'What a super idea!' I exclaimed. 'Where's the local paper? Let's see when there's going to be a meet near enough for us to hack to.'

'Perhaps Jan and Susan would come out with us, too,' suggested Pip, while I searched the sports pages of the paper. 'Where's the meet on Saturday?'

'It's at Islip Saturday and Nuneaton Tuesday' I said. 'I'm sure we could hack to Islip easily, it can't be more than five miles. Do let's go.'

We did go hunting on Saturday, and in fact we soon became

157

so keen that no one else in the household got a chance to see the local paper when it arrived, until Pip and I had pored over it to determine whether we could possibly hunt the coming week-end. If we could, all our plans revolved around our day with hounds. Jan and Susan often came out with us, and Bishop, particularly, proved to be a wonderful hunter.

Pip had looked forward to hunting April for so long that I would like to be able to record that she proved to be a perfect hunter, but I'm afraid Life isn't like that. April was certainly very fast and kept Pip well up to the front, but she was unmanageable in a snaffle, and even with a pelham and the added leaverage of a curb chain, she was not at all easy to hold. There was one terrible day when everything seemed to go badly. The Field Master had somehow lost hounds and led us full tilt down a narrow, muddy lane, only to change his mind a few moments later, pull up sharply, and turn about ready to retrace his steps. At that moment April's curb chain broke and Pip, now totally out of control, went flying on, coming to rest, finally, with a sickening thud against the ample hind quarters of the Colonel's horse. The air was extremely blue for several minutes until some of the kinder members of the hunt realized what Pip's problem was and helped us to improvise a curb chain out of string. Despite a few such inevitable black moments, we had some wonderful days out with hounds and April jumped like a stag when hounds were running, and sped across the ground like lightning whenever Pip gave her the chance, leaving me and Charm panting along behind.

We did not neglect the other ponies during the winter but we realized now that Shandy had grown as large as she was ever going to grow. She was obviously never going to be a very useful pony to us, since we were both nearly six feet tall!

'Even if we married terribly young and had children right away it really isn't an economic proposition to keep Shandy for them' said Pip one day. So we both faced up squarely to the inevitable fact that we must school Shandy and then sell her to the best home we could find.

From the time she was a foal I had known that Shandy was my responsibility and I worked hard on her schooling all spring, giving Charm a well-earned rest out on the Meadow. I was too old now to compete in Juvenile classes, but Pip would show jump Charm during the coming season, so she needed a rest after her season's hunting before showing began in earnest.

Shandy was mildly surprised the day I first mounted her, but not at all resentful, and she proved to be an apt pupil, quickly learning to respond to the pressures of my legs and hands. I did not ride her for longer than half an hour at a time, as I felt I was much too big for her, but that seemed to be sufficient to turn her into a useful little pony in a matter of three or four months. When I felt sure that she was a safe and quiet ride for a reasonably competent child, I advertised her in the local paper and finally sold her to a very nice family who lived about twenty miles away.

I think it was selling Shandy that finally made us realize that Molly was simply rotting away out on the Meadow when she might have been leading an active and useful life. We were all much too big and heavy to ride her now, and even Jan, who was a petite sort of person, had outgrown her and felt more comfortable riding Bishop. We all knew we couldn't possibly sell Molly – she was too much one of the family. But one evening Father came home and asked 'What would you girls think of the suggestion that we might consider giving Molly away to a very good home? No, don't jump at me with all those objections' – as we started to make horrified criticisms – 'think about it calmly for a moment. I know a farming family who live at Great Tew, about thirty miles from here. They are charming people who are used to animals and know how to look after them. They have two little boys, small and light, seven and nine years old, and very sensibly, they are looking for an old pony who will teach the boys to ride and be a safe and sensible companion for them. Now, what do you both think?'

We discussed the possibilities for Molly's future in much the same way that we had discussed buying her in the first place, naming her foals, and finding her a place to live during the time she had been with us. If we gave Molly to the two little boys there was no doubt that she would have a good home, and wouldn't she enjoy it more than simply being turned out on the Meadow for the rest of her life? Knowing how she loved children we couldn't possibly doubt that she would enjoy teaching the boys to ride; enjoy building their confidence by carrying them smoothly on her gentle back if they were nervous; and enjoy dumping them on the soft turf if they got a little above themselves and tried to show off. All things considered, it began to seem almost heartless to deprive Molly of the benefit of joining a loving family who really needed her. She would have her own paddock and orchard close to the farm house, and she would certainly have things easier than fending for herself through another wind swept winter on Port Meadow.

The decision was finally made, and although it was hard we were sure it was right. One day early in the summer, Molly's new family sent a horse box to the Wolvercote stables, and a gleaming, well-brushed dark brown pony with a broad white blaze and big, gentle eyes, once more left that stable yard for a new home and a new life. Molly was loved and cared for by her new family just as much as she was loved by us. Whenever we could we went to visit her on Sunday afternoons, and we were always met with a happy whinney and pricked ears as she came to the gate for her carrots. She remained healthy and active for four more years and when, one windy autumn day, after she had been running a temperature and having difficulty breathing for two or three days, the veterinarian said she had pneumonia and there was little hope, her days were brought to a merciful end, quietly and without pain, in her own pasture, close to the house and the family that was then her own family.